MINIATURES
How to Make Them, Use Them, Sell Them

MINIATURES
How to Make Them, Use Them, Sell Them

PHYLLIS MÉRAS

Illustrated with Photographs and Drawings

HOUGHTON MIFFLIN COMPANY

BOSTON 1976

Books by Phyllis Méras
First Spring: A Martha's Vineyard Journal
A Yankee Way with Wood
Miniatures
How to Make Them, Use Them, Sell Them

Book design by Sandra Starr Lahan

The drawings in *Miniatures* are by Mark Mulhall and Barbara Taylor Hackney

Library of Congress Cataloging in Publication Data
Méras, Phyllis.
Miniatures: how to make them, use them, sell them.
1. Miniature craft.   I. Title.
TT178.M47   745.59'2   76-16493
ISBN 0-395-24344-0

Printed in the United States of America

A 10 9 8 7 6 5 4 3 2 1

To
Donald and Mia Bess,
Rebecca, Francesca, and Pamela
and in memory of
Teddy

acknowledgments

Only the assistance of many accomplished miniaturists, collectors of miniatures, and dealers in miniatures have made this book possible.

Particularly helpful in the gathering, organizing, and revising of material have been James P. Harrell of the National Association of Miniature Enthusiasts, Kathryn Falk of Mini Mundus, Dorothy Lindquist and Mary Sheldon of the Woman's Exchange of Hingham, Massachusetts, Sandy Verrill of the Depot Gallery in Concord, Massachusetts, Mary Alley, Mary Carraher, Fran Cook, Claire Danos, Judy Faulkner, Elizabeth Fisher, Larry Garnett, Joe Hermes, Paul Jedjezek, Lit Lapsley, Anne Mitchell, Ted Norton, B. Jean Silva, Susan Sirkis, Dee Snyder, George Tait, Bettyanne Twigg, and Pamela White.

Providing advice on woodworking techniques were Richard Benjamin, John E. Méras, Robert Mussey, and Dr. John E. Wallace.

Peter Chowka, Robert F. McCrystal, Alison Shaw, Thomas D. Stevens, and Robert Tobey kindly offered their aid in the developing and printing of pictures.

And patient support throughout this project came from Douglas N. Riggs and Donald Alden of the Providence *Journal*, and from Frances Tenenbaum of Houghton Mifflin.

note

Unless exact measurements are specified, the drawings in this book are not to scale. For miniaturists, the standard reduction is 1 foot equals 1 inch.

contents

This dining room sideboard is by Donald Buttfield and is a good example of the detailed and authentic work done by master miniaturists. (Photography Unlimited)

CHAPTER 1

WELCOME TO A MINIATURE WORLD

☙ Strollers on New York City's Lexington Avenue on a Saturday afternoon have been heard to ask "What's the commotion?" and hurry along curiously to see why so many passersby are peering into the window of Mini Mundus, a small, unpretentious shop between 73rd and 74th streets.

Smallness is exactly the answer. Mini Mundus—small world—sells miniature things: cabbages the size of marbles; clocks that work though they're no bigger than a thumbnail; knitted objects so minuscule that they must be worked on straight pins; jigsaw puzzles that would fit on top of a large postage stamp.

All over the country the same phenomenon can be seen—large crowds drawn by tiny objects, for collecting miniatures is one of the most popular hobbies in the country today. And it is the natural parent of the newest, fastest-growing craft—making miniatures.

Anyone with imagination can make miniatures. One of the most appealing aspects of the craft is that you can approach it from any direction, out of any interest.

Do you haunt garage sales and auctions? Are you a button collector? Gewgaws from flea markets—old postcards and belt buckles and cigar boxes, brooches and lace and trinkets—become landscape paintings and picture frames, mini-cash registers, and curtains in the miniature world. Buttons become bed warmers and saucers and paperweights.

If you're handy with a needle, you can make petit point rugs and tiny samplers. If you like to work in wood, there is always furniture to be made—simple country pieces or sophisticated Hepplewhite and Queen Anne and Chippendale in walnut or mahogany or cherry.

If you're thinking of selling your house now that the children are grown, make a miniature of it to treasure.

For the amateur sculptor or ceramist there are offbeat satisfactions aplenty in sculpting mini-busts for mini-tables and mini-apples for mini-fruit bowls, or throwing mini-pots.

The old bead necklaces that Grandmother wore, but you never will, can be transformed with a little beading wire or thread into the most elegant of chandeliers.

No one is certain how many miniature-makers there are in the country today, but there are well over 6000 serious collectors, and since collectors often turn to mini-making when they cannot find an object they need, there are certainly thousands of craftsmen of miniatures, too. These craftsmen, as you will see, are often turning a profit from their hobby. And there's no reason why you can't too.

Amid today's complexities, psychiatrists say, a miniature world is a manageable one—hence the upsurge of interest in miniatures. Take advantage of it!

If you like fine furniture, but can't afford to ship a houseful of antiques across the country each time a move is made, create the pieces you would like to own in miniature. Miniatures are easy to pack.

The frustrated decorator will find all the work he wants selecting the perfect upholstery pattern for a miniature sofa, finding the right draperies to match, a carpet that blends, wallpaper that highlights the furnishings, and the art and bric-a-brac that complete any setting.

Enthusiasm for the mini-world has become so great in the past half-dozen years that three national periodicals, one international periodical, and many regional ones, have been started to advise the aficionado about where to buy what he needs for his hobby.

To facilitate buying and selling, there are annually shows and sales by the hundreds. Carriage World, a shop selling miniatures in Scotch Plains, New Jersey, held a series of outdoor fairs for miniature buyers and makers one summer and from June to September averaged 500 customers each Sunday.

The directors of the prestigious Parke-Bernet Gallery in New York found miniature-collecting an exciting enough trend recently to hold the gallery's first auction of miniatures.

Everywhere, shops for collectors and craftsmen are sprouting, and shops that once had miniatures or miniature-making components only as a side line now give priority to miniatures.

The Woman's Exchange in Hingham, Massachusetts, in operation since 1958, and carrying needlepoint, stuffed toys, and handwork of all kinds, now makes more than 50 per cent of its revenue from miniatures and materials for miniature-making, though they occupy less than a third of the shop space.

At the Pink Sleigh in Oldwick, New Jersey, a store that began as a Christmas shop twenty years ago, one whole end of the building has had to be devoted to materials for miniaturists. It's almost as easy today to find a shop with a name like Small World, Mini Things, Wee'uns, Wee Little Studio, Isn't It (a small world), as it is to find an ordinary gift shop.

Such hobby shop items as découpage spray, quilling paper, model airplane glues and paints, ties for miniature railroads, hardware for ship models are often out of stock because of the demand from miniature-makers.

All sorts of people are miniature-buyers and -makers. Last year thirty of them visited England on a "miniatour" to view such world-famous collections as those of Queen Mary and the wife of the novelist Graham Greene. Two American collectors of note are the former child actresses Shirley Temple Black and Jane Withers.

Robert V. Dankanics, who builds dollhouses and sells mini-bricks, mini-wainscoting, mini-flooring, and many other mini things at his Doll House Factory in Lebanon, New Jersey, gasps at the increase of interest in the Lilliputian world in the three years he has been in the business.

*An all-purpose motor tool will make furniture,
chamfer, drill and sand. With a pocketknife or an
X-acto, it can fashion all sorts of miniature objects.
(Richard Benjamin)*

CHAPTER 2

TOOLS

It's hard to think of a craft or hobby that requires a smaller investment in tools and equipment than miniature-making. Which, since proportion is what miniatures are all about, is as it should be. Even if you've never worked a drill press or owned a lathe, you can create beautiful reproductions of furniture and household accessories. With a little patience, you can make exquisite turnings with emery boards and files. X-acto knives and single-edge razor blades will do most of your cutting satisfactorily. Many of the "tools" the instructions in this book call for are everyday household items, such as toothpicks, Q-Tips, emery boards, and pencils.

But if you want a well-stocked workshop, here is a complete list of miniaturist's tools, compiled by Dorothy Lindquist of the Woman's Exchange in Hingham, Massachusetts, who makes the miniatures she sells on a work space the size of a kitchen table. Exclusive of the power equipment you may eventually want to buy, she estimates that $35 will cover the cost of all the tools you'll need.

A miniature maker's work table need not take up much room. Elspeth's is an example.

FOR MAKING HOLES

1. Awl
2. Ice pick
3. Ticket punch from a stationery store
4. Ratchet drill from a hardware store
5. Pin vise drill from a hardware store
6. Common, straight, and eye pins from a sewing or craft supply store

FOR SMOOTHING

1. Gesso or any wood filler from a craft supply store
2. Model airplane dope from a craft supply store
3. Flo-Quil sealer from a craft supply shop
4. Découpage sealer from a craft supply shop
5. Scotchguard to seal bread dough items
6. Spray varnish

POWER TOOLS

1. Dremel Moto-Tool with attachments
2. Unimat
3. McGraw-Edison Shopmate
4. Jeweler's lathe
5. Jigsaw
6. Dentist's drill from dental supply house
7. Electric drill with various bits

FOR CUTTING

1. X-acto knife with No. 10 and No. 11 blades, available at any craft supply store
2. Mat knife from an art store for cutting curves
3. X-acto razor saw from a craft supply store
4. Wire clippers from a hardware store
5. Tin snips from a hardware store
6. Scissors of various sizes

FOR FINE WORK

1. Surgical tweezers from a medical supply store .
2. Needle-nose pliers from a hardware store
3. A magnifying glass
4. Toothpicks and Q-Tips
5. A hypodermic needle from a drugstore for getting glue into small places
6. Dental tools from a dental supply store

FOR DRAWING AND DECORATING

1. Good quality artists' paintbrushes in various sizes
2. Felt-tipped colored pens and markers
3. Indelible colored pens
4. Fine-point pens
5. Lead pencils
6. Colored pencils
7. Acrylic paints, Martin-Senour Williamsburg paints, Flo-Quil paints from a crafts supply shop
8. Nail polish remover for cleaning
9. Hair spray for stiffening
10. Varnish, shellac, or Minwax for finishing
11. Minwax for staining

FOR JOINING

1. White glue like Elmer's Glue-All or Grippit to glue wood to wood, cloth to wood
2. Sobo glue to glue fabric to wood
3. Epoxy to glue metal to metal or metal to wood
4. Weldit to glue wood to glass
5. Wallpaper paste

6. Veneer glue, Contact cement or Ambroid glue for laying floors
7. A propane torch from the hardware store. Micronox is used by many miniature-makers
8. Soldering iron, solder, and flux
9. Wire from an electrical or electronics supply house
10. Straight pins and eye pins from a jewelry findings store

FOR TURNING

1. Files from a hardware store
2. Emery boards from a drugstore
3. Sandpaper from a hardware store (including the finest grain you can find for final work)
4. 0000 steel wool from a hardware store for buffing after sanding
5. Kelly clamps from a medical supply house for holding work
6. Paper clips and paper clamps from a stationery store
7. Rag to remove steel wool dust

FOR PERFECT CORNERS AND LEVEL TOPS

1. T-square from an art supply store
2. X-acto miter box from a craft supply store
3. Miniature level from a craft supply store
4. Several steel-edged rulers, 6" to 18"
5. Draftsman's triangle

FOR HAMMERING

1. Tack hammer from a hardware store

A detail of one shelf of Fenner Wheeler's bookcase setting. (Richard Benjamin)

CHAPTER 3

An old-fashioned flour measure makes this choice set-
ting for Jane and Earl Fahlquist's miniatures. In
Barrington, Rhode Island, where the Fahlquists live,
flour measures aren't easy to find, but they never
pass a country antique shop on their travels without
stopping to look for a measure. (Richard Benjamin)

CONTAINERS

So you want to make miniatures? What will you put them in? A dollhouse is the obvious answer, but by no means the only one. And certainly not necessary if you are a beginning miniaturist and not sure in what direction your interest and skill will lead you.

If you don't want to build or buy a container, a discarded TV cabinet can be transformed into an attractive room setting. Old-fashioned milk crates, wooden cheese boxes, fish tanks, ecology boxes, printer's type trays, and deep bureau drawers can all be used with a little ingenuity. An empty bookcase, especially the Victorian glass-fronted kind, a corner cupboard, the compartments of a desk, a liquor cabinet, or a hanging wall cabinet are settings that are almost ready-made. From an old German spice cabinet, one miniature-maker fashioned a charming town house. You can even use a table top or mantelpiece to display a few of your best pieces.

Some miniature-makers like driftwood as the base for an old-fashioned scene. Cigar boxes, shoeboxes, and cardboard cartons have been used for generations for simple settings (though furniture for a cigar box will be smaller than the 1 inch to 1 foot scale furniture and accessories we'll be talking about here). If you've always wanted to live in a castle, try combining a tubular oatmeal or salt box with a cardboard carton. And a hollow log is an old standby for a family of mini-mice or mini-bears or mini-frogs.

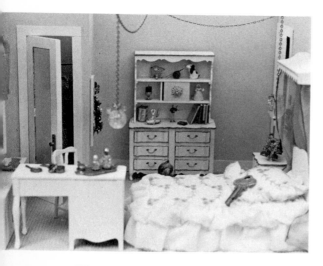

When Mary Carraher's daughter was married and moved to her own home, Mrs. Carraher reproduced the bedroom of her girlhood in miniature for her.

Actually, all that's needed as a setting for miniatures is a flat surface. Ideally, of course, you will have walls, too, so they can be painted or papered and hung with pictures and mirrors for a more effective room. Here is the setting Mary Carraher of Oak Park, Illinois, makes:

ROOM BOX INSTRUCTIONS

1. When you have decided on the size of your room, cut the walls, floor and ceiling from ¼-inch basswood plywood using a table saw.

2. Sand the boards with #220 sandpaper and wipe clean with a lint-free cloth. Seal with a commercial sealer or make a 50/50 sealer by mixing ½ pint Bulls Eye shellac and ½ pint denatured alcohol. Store mixture in an airtight container and shake thoroughly before using. Apply with a lint-free cloth and wipe across the wood. Allow to dry. (If you choose to stain the outside of the box instead of painting, the sealer is applied after stain has dried.)

3. Assemble the box room, resting the walls on the floor pieces and the ceiling on the walls.

4. Drill small holes for screws where you will join the walls together. For the actual joining, use either #17 wire brads, 1 inch long, or #1 flathead screws, 1 inch long.

5. Stain or paint the outside of the box as desired. Allow eight hours for it to dry. Cover with a satin or semi-gloss varnish and allow the box to dry for another eight hours.

6. Paper or paint its interior as you desire.

A ROOM WITH A VIEW

If you want a room with a view, you will need an inner partition of ⅛-inch illustration board at the back of your room.

1. With a razor blade knife, using a steel ruler as a guide (preferably one with a cork back to prevent slipping), cut the illustration board to the exact measurements, wall-to-wall and ceiling-to-floor, of the interior of your room setting. Do your cutting on a large piece of plywood or Masonite to protect the table surface. Be sure to stand up when you are cutting, to keep the knife square with the illustration board.

2. Draw any window or door that you wish on graph paper, using the scale of 1 inch equals 1 foot.

3. Transfer the window and door measurements to the illustration board and cut the openings.

4. Once the openings are cut, they must be framed. For this, use $1/16$ by ⅛-inch balsa wood strips that have been sanded, stained, and sealed before they are cut.

5. Using a #2 X-acto knife and a #24 blade, cut the vertical sides of the frame first (that part of the frame that is inset—where weights hang in some windows). Do the cutting on a piece of wood or Masonite and use a sawing motion since balsa wood is quite soft and too much pressure will crush it.

6. Put Sobo glue on the ⅛-inch side of the balsa and glue the wooden strips flush into the opening in the illustration board.

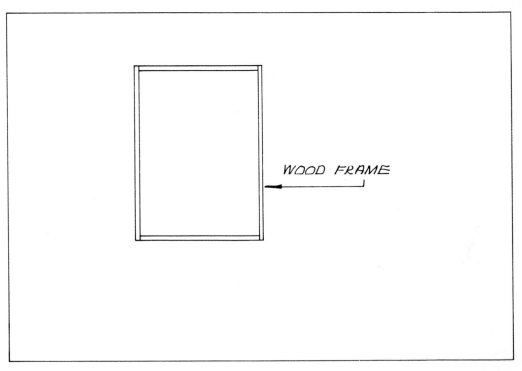

WOOD FRAME

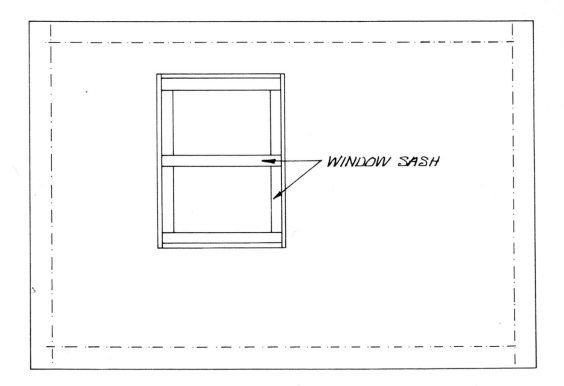

WINDOW SASH

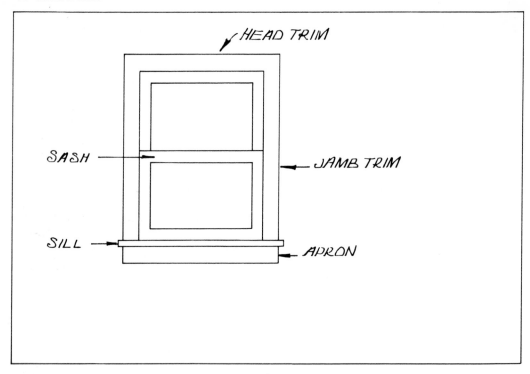

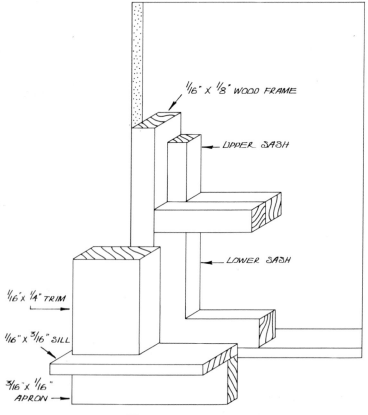

ISOMETRIC SECTION OF WINDOW UNIT

7. Cut the two horizontal pieces for the top and bottom of the inner frame and glue them, similarly, into the illustration board opening.

8. If you wish double-hung windows, build the sashes from balsa strips. Remember that the lower sash moves up and down in front of the upper sash, so you must glue the lower sash on the room side of the jamb (the inset frame you have just glued into place). Even though you have only the ⅛-inch thickness of the jamb with which to work, the difference in the depths of the upper and lower sashes will be noticeable.

9. Divide the window height in half. Make the lower sash first, cutting the lower horizontal pieces from a ³/₁₆ by ¹/₁₆-inch balsa wood strip. Put Sobo glue on the ¹/₁₆-inch edge and glue it to the front half of the jamb.

10. Measure and cut the sides from ³/₁₆ by ¹/₁₆-inch balsa. Put Sobo glue on the ¹/₁₆-inch edges and glue the pieces in place.

11. The centerpiece, or the top horizontal piece of the lower sash is cut from a ⅛ by ¹/₁₆-inch balsa wood strip. It should be the same length as the bottom of the sash and will rest (and be glued) on the top of the sides of the sash. When it is in place, make the upper sash in the same manner, using the back half of the jamb. (Examine a window in your own home while you are doing this.) Glue the centerpiece of the upper sash directly behind the centerpiece of the bottom sash. You are now ready to trim the rest of the window opening.

12. Use ¼ by ¹/₁₆-inch balsa wood strips for the woodwork that goes around the window and trim as shown. Miter the top corners. The sill is cut from a ³/₁₆ by ¹/₁₆-inch balsa wood strip and extends on either side of the window opening. Glue it perpendicular to the illustration board.

13. The apron is below the sill and is cut from a ³/₁₆ by ¹/₁₆-inch balsa wood strip. Glue it to the illustration board as shown.

14. Cut the glass for the window from Shrink-Art plastic or use the plastic lid from a stationery box. Cut the glass slightly larger than the window frame and glue it to the back of the illustration board with Sobo glue.

15. Now wallpaper or paint the illustration board partition. You can give the wall a stucco-like finish by applying a thick layer of glue with a pallet or butter knife and then sprinkling on Kitty Litter. Or use gesso and salt and pepper; gesso and pebbles; acrylic paint and salt and pepper; or acrylic paint and sand. Let the wall dry and spray it with a fixative.

Driftwood is the base for this miniature setting of Betsy Ross, at the Pink Sleigh in Oldwick, New Jersey.

The Mark Sagendorfs of Fairfield, Connecticut, design this three-story town house for miniature collectors.

BUTTRESSING A PARTITION

Should you have decided on a room with a partition through which you can see "landscape" glued to the outer wall, you will need to buttress and support the partition in the room box. For this purpose, use ½ by ½-inch pine parting stops.

1. Cut parting stops with a coping saw. Never use a buttress that is less than ½ inch

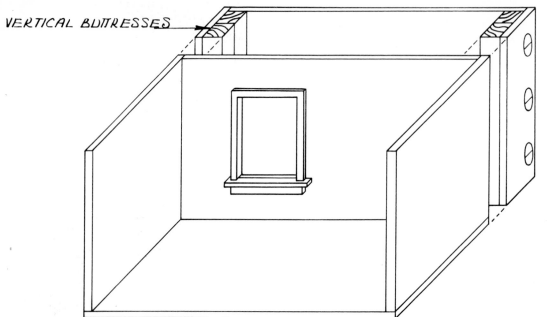

VERTICAL BUTTRESSES

ROOM BOX SHOWN WITH ILLUSTRATION BOARD PARTITION IN PLACE.
VERTICAL BUTTRESSES ARE BEHIND IT.

in depth. If you wish considerable depth between the partition and the back wall, stack two or more parting stops to achieve the desired depth. Glue them in place with Sobo glue. Glue partition to them.

2. Be sure in selecting a picture for the wall outside the partition that it is big enough so that no part of the actual back wall can be seen through the window. Select a print. Glue it first with Sobo glue to a piece of lightweight cardboard cut to fit against the inside of your outer wall. Spray it, front and back, with a clear fixative (such as Tuffilm or Blair) before gluing. Glue it in place with Sobo.

CEILINGS AND WALLS

If you want to add special touches to your ceilings and walls, you can purchase baseboard and moldings for miniatures and glue them around the edges of your room. For a beamed ceiling, glue strips of stained basswood to your ceiling with Sobo. If you like Victorian plaster ceilings, cut paper doilies to make the decorative ceiling corners or cut a small circle from the doily to make a center-

of-the-room highlight from which a chandelier may be hung. After gluing these doily pieces in place, gesso and paint them to make them an integral part of the room.

1. Wallpapering should be done next. First, prime or seal the walls to be papered. Flat wall paint, varnish, shellac or Glutoline wall sizing will do as sealers, says California miniature wallpaper designer Joe Hermes. Don't use glossy enamel, for paper will not adhere to it, he warns.

2. If you have decided not to have an inner partition of illustration board with a window in your setting, be sure to sand down any lumps that there may be in the wooden outer walls that will be your only walls. Use shellac to seal in any color or stains in the walls that might bleed through the paper when it is wet. Then proceed with the actual papering.

3. Dollhouse paper is readily available in many delicate designs (Joe Hermes has more than sixty of them), and they are sure to make an attractive room. But if you prefer to do it all yourself, Italian marbelized paper or Cockerel paper, heavy gift wrapping paper

Rob Lyon of Essex, Connecticut, a student at William and Mary College in Virginia, planked and paneled this room.

with a small design, or good quality typing paper onto which you have stenciled a design can be used.

To make your own stencil, cut a design—pineapples, urns, eagles, hearts, and bells were all popular in Colonial times—in an art gum eraser. Leave the design raised so it will be like an ordinary rubber stamp. Make your own stamp pad of several thicknesses of paper towels, or use a commercial one. Pour light-colored poster paints onto the pad. Wet the eraser in it and print your design up and down on 20 or 24 bond paper.

4. Wallpaper paste is best for applying mini-papers. Mix two or three tablespoons of paste into enough water to bring the mixture to the consistency of melted ice cream. Use a blender to remove any lumps, or keep the mixture in the refrigerator overnight—the lumps will dissolve by themselves. An empty milk carton with the top cut off makes a good container. Use a ½-inch brush to apply the paste.

5. To fit the paper around a fireplace or a window, cut it into sections and apply it piece by piece, carefully matching the pattern.

6. Put the paste both on the wallpaper and on the walls. With a little rubber roller or wadded paper towel, press out any air bubbles or wrinkles.

THE FLOOR

The bottom of your room setting can now be carpeted, or the flooring laid. If you use carpeting, a light-weight double-knit fabric is effective.

1. Apply Sobo glue evenly but not too thickly to the bottom. Let it dry until tacky. Then press the cloth into place. The glue will hold the carpeting to the wood and shrink it into line, making it tight.

2. If you prefer boards that show, use basswood, balsa, or pine strips of random widths and lengths, stained the color you wish before they are glued into place. Don't use plywood, however, for it takes stain badly. Minwax is a good stain for this purpose. If you like, make simulated nail holes in the corners of the planks with a tiny nail.

3. Veneer and veneer tape are other possibilities as flooring materials. If you select veneer, be sure that you use Constantine's veneer glue or the veneer will not lie straight. To prevent warping, cut short rather than long pieces of veneer. If you use veneer tape, which is easily cut with scissors, apply it with Contact cement. When you use the tape, it is easy to mix different grains and colors.

4. You can also try making a parquet. To do this effectively, make an exact drawing of your floor space and then figure out mathematically how you would like your parquet arranged. "Stained basswood squares make the best parquet," says Pamela White of Boston, who has a special fondness for them. "Put Ambroid glue on one section of the floor, glue down a section of parquet, weight it down, and proceed to the next section."

5. If your setting is a kitchen or shop or a very modern room, you might want to use a square (and a bit more) of thin vinyl floor tile in a small pattern, or the mosaic tile used for patio tables.

Now you are ready to furnish your room.

This mosaic tile ordinarily used for full-scale patio tables becomes flooring for a miniature Georgian entrance hall in the hands of Pamela White of Boston. (Andrew Grainger)

In this glass-front bookcase, Fenner Wheeler of West
Mystic, Connecticut, has arranged a variety of miniature displays. (Richard Benjamin)

This toucan was hand-painted in a miniature book by Rob Lyon of Essex, Connecticut. (Richard Benjamin)

CHAPTER 4

An elegant ballroom chandelier begins, like many other miniature lighting fixtures, with jewelry findings. (J. Kender)

In the real world, accessories are the final touch, the last thing to make or buy to complete a room setting. For a beginning miniature-maker, however, the accessory department is a good place to shop for a first project. Accessories are often easy, always fun, and of endless variety.

LIGHTING FIXTURES

The lights in your miniature room can be candles, chandeliers, hurricane lamps, courting or "Gone With the Wind" lamps, sconces, or modern table lamps.

In a Victorian setting, a Tiffany lamp is always appropriate and is simple to make:

TIFFANY HANGING LAMP

1. With a pin, prick a Ping-Pong ball in the middle. (This lets the air out of the ball, making it easier to cut.)

2. Make an incision with the sharpest X-acto knife blade you have, where the pin

ACCESSORIES

A Ping-Pong ball cut in two with cuticle scissors was the start of this miniature Tiffany lamp. (Peter Schaaf for Mini Mundus)

prick was. Continue your cut so the ball is in two halves. (One Ping-Pong ball makes two shades.) If you like, you can scallop the bottom of the shade by cutting it with cuticle scissors.

3. In pencil, draw a design on the outside of the half-ball.

4. With glass stain bought in a hobby shop, paint the "glass" sections of the shade. Let the stain dry for twenty-four hours.

5. With opaque acrylic paint, outline the glass sections. The opaque paint will resemble the lead that holds the glass in place in a genuine Tiffany lamp. Let it dry for twenty-four hours.

6. Once the opaque paint is thoroughly dry, cover the entire shade with spray gloss fixative as a finish coat. It is available in art and hobby shops.

7. Make a hole in the top of the painted shade with a pin. Run a piece of the craft wire used in flower-making through the hole. On the inside of the shade, attach the wire to a medium-sized white or yellow bead, which will represent the light bulb. Do this by poking Sobo glue into the hole in the bead with a toothpick, and then inserting the wire. Where the wire emerges from the top of the shade, insert it through a bead cap. (Jewelry findings, like bead caps and pieces of discarded jewelry from your own drawers provide the makings for all sorts of miniature lighting fixtures.)

8. Lift the finding enough to put Sobo glue under it to attach it to the shade.

9. With your fingers, or with needle-nose pliers, twist the end of the craft wire through the last link of a fine chain, which will be used to attach the lamp to the ceiling.

A Victorian chandelier with hand-blown glass globes.
(Peter Schaaf for Mini Mundus)

Jewelry findings, painted beads, plastic tubing are
combined in these "Gone With the Wind" lamps.
(Peter Schaaf for Mini Mundus)

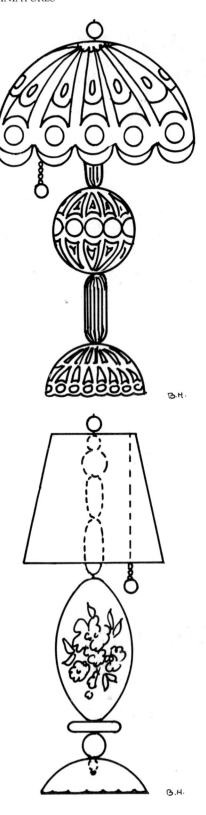

VICTORIAN TABLE LAMP

Victorian table lamps can be made entirely of jewelry findings. Barbara Taylor Hackney of New York City uses Sobo glue to link the parts of this one together:

1. For the lamp base, run glue along a jeweler's long, head-type pin, and slip onto it an anchor bead for the base and a large filigree bead above that.

2. For the shade, use one very large filigree bead cap.

3. For the pull, attach a small crystal bead to a length of fine chain.

MODERN TABLE LAMP

Make this lamp in the same way, by sliding beads of various sizes and shapes along a long, head-type jeweler's pin. Instead of the filigree bead cap, make a lamp shade from a large toothpaste tube (or similar) cap.

EASY CHANDELIER

A simple but attractive chandelier is made from bent cup hooks inserted and glued into tiny holes drilled into the wooden piece that tops a dime-store flag. Paint the screw ends white to simulate twisted candles. If you want plain candles, cut the ends off, and glue on candle-length pieces of coat hanger wire with epoxy. Paint them white.

Jewelry findings, beads, a tube cap, and a piece of chain combine to make a painted ceramic lamp (left) designed by Barbara Taylor Hackney of New York City. The Victorian table lamp at right, by the same designer, is also constructed of beads and findings. (J. Kender)

Cup hooks, links of chain, and the top of a five-and-ten-cent store toy flag inspired B. Jean Silva of West Tisbury, Massachusetts, to create this simple chandelier.

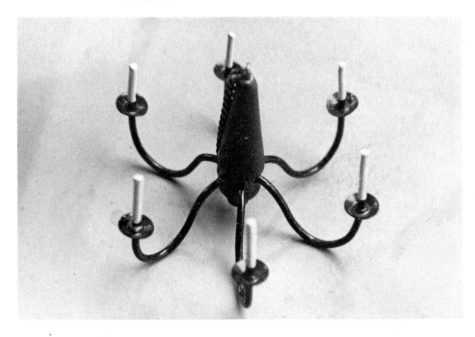

CHANDELIER ARM

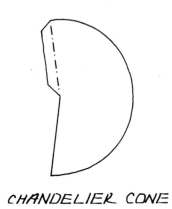

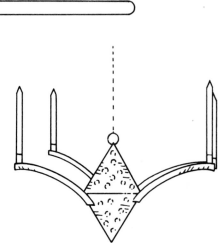

CHANDELIER CONE

SUSAN SIRKIS' CHANDELIER

SUSAN SIRKIS' CHANDELIER

1. Cut two pieces of brass shim or flattened tin can with tin snips in the accompanying pattern.

2. Form each piece into a cone, gluing with epoxy. Then, with more epoxy, glue the two cone-shaped pieces together at the wide ends of the cones.

3. Cut four arm patterns from brass shim or tin. Glue them in place evenly around the center of the two joined cones. Glue small eyelets on top at the end of each arm.

4. Paint round toothpicks white with black tips to make candles. Glue into eyelets.

5. Glue a jewelry jump ring to the top of the chandelier with epoxy. Attach a piece of chain to the jump ring.

6. Paint the entire assemblage with flat black model paint or use silver paint to represent tin.

BALLROOM CHANDELIER

You can make an elegant crystal ballroom chandelier from your beads and jewelry findings.

Materials
A length of chain with a jump ring
A long eye-type jeweler's pin
A dozen or so elongated filigree bead caps
  (for candle holders and finial)

B.H.

Two sizes of faceted glass beads
A large filigree bead
A faceted glass teardrop
A dozen or so small glass beads (for candle
  tips)
Round toothpicks (for candles)
A small filigree bead
A large filigree wheel
Many glass seed beads (for stringing
  festoons)

1. Spread epoxy lightly along the eye pin. With the help of tweezers, assemble the number and variety of beads you like on the pin, as well as the large and small filigree beads (with an assortment of beads separating them).

2. Put the large filigree bead just under the large filigree wheel. Remember, in making your assembly, that the pin "eye" must be at the top.

3. Clip off the excess pin when you have arranged the beads, and glue the teardrop to the bottom bead.

4. String the seed beads on the beading thread, and attach them in festoons around the filigree wheels. Glue them or tie them with thread that you conceal under the beads.

5. Assemble the candles (the round toothpicks painted white) and the holders (the elongated filigree bead caps) and glue them at intervals around the larger filigree wheels.

6. Attach an attractive chain to the eye at the top of the chandelier.

CANDLES

If the idea of round toothpicks as the candles in your glittering chandelier seems too plebeian, you can make real candles in miniature. Melt a small quantity of candle wax in a beaker (old candle ends will do). Attach a thread or two to a pencil and dip the thread into the molten wax for two seconds. Remove and let harden. Repeat until wax buildup reaches the desired thickness (about 1/16-inch). Trim the wicks. But beware— candles made in this purist way may droop if your room setting is left in the sun. An easier way to put genuine wax in your chandeliers and candlesticks is to use cut-off birthday cake candles.

If you're not a purist, matchsticks, hatpins,

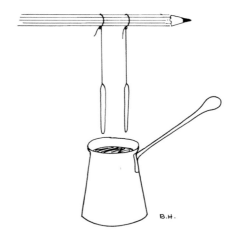

or wire dipped in gesso make imitation candles as satisfactory as round toothpicks. You can also cut white typewriter paper into strips. The width of the strip is the length of the candle. Put a piece of black thread (the wick) across the paper and hold it in place with a dot of glue. Then roll the paper into a tiny tight roll, gluing it as you go.

CANDLESTICK

Run a large cup sequin halfway down a nail. Glue the bottom of the nail to an eyelet, a grommet or a snap—whichever looks better with the size nail you are using. Paint the candlestick from the sequin on down with gold acrylic paint. Paint the candle half of the nail white. This is another suggestion from Susan Sirkis, of West Point, New York, who publishes "The Wish Booklets" for miniaturists and doll-makers.

HURRICANE LAMP

Those miniature goblets that gift shops sell as party favors make the chimneys for hurricane lamps. Glass beads and bead caps make bases, and the parts are arranged on a jeweler's flat-based pin.

1. Set the flat end of the pin on your workbench or table. Apply any white glue or epoxy to the pin and slide the bead cap on first to make the lamp bottom.

2. If necessary, apply a little more glue and slide on the glass bead.

3. Then slide on a bead cap.

4. With a hot pin, burn a hole in the bottom of the goblet large enough to slip the pin through. Tom Devereaux of Chicago sets Italian wax matches inside the goblet of his lamps. This is especially effective, but if you don't have access to Italian matches, you can use your tiny matchstick or toothpick candles.

SCONCE

If you'd like a Colonial effect in your room setting, try making sconces from the backs of screw earrings (look at one sometime). Cut the screw apart and remove it. Bend the plate the jewel is ordinarily attached to so that it is perpendicular to the stem. Glue half of an empty medicine capsule to the plate to hold your candle.

PICTURES

Attractively framed pictures are part of what makes a house a home, and it's always difficult to decide what sorts of pictures to hang. Postage stamps, wildlife stamps, cut-outs from magazines, and famous paintings (or sections of famous paintings) cut from museum postcard reproductions are among the pictures most frequently hung in rooms full of miniatures. But pieces of the backs of old playing cards (especially those with linenlike texture), old Valentines, old sheets of music, and heads from family snapshots can also be used.

OIL PAINTINGS

If you really want to make a miniature landscape look as if it is a genuine oil, remove the picture from the face of the card or magazine with Decal-it, then glue it onto muslin or buckram to provide texture and onto a white index card to provide backing. When it is ready to be framed, coat it with spray découpage or medium acrylic gloss to darken it a little.

Mini-art is attractively framed by Dee Snyder of North Palm Beach, Florida, with Popsicle sticks and découpage foil.

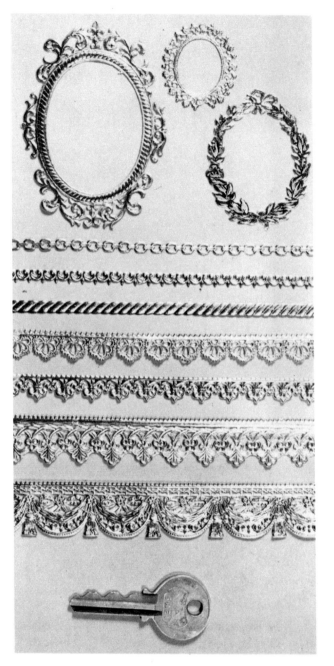

Gilt-embossed paper, like this from Brandon Memorabilia, can be used to decorate miniature picture frames. (J. Kender)

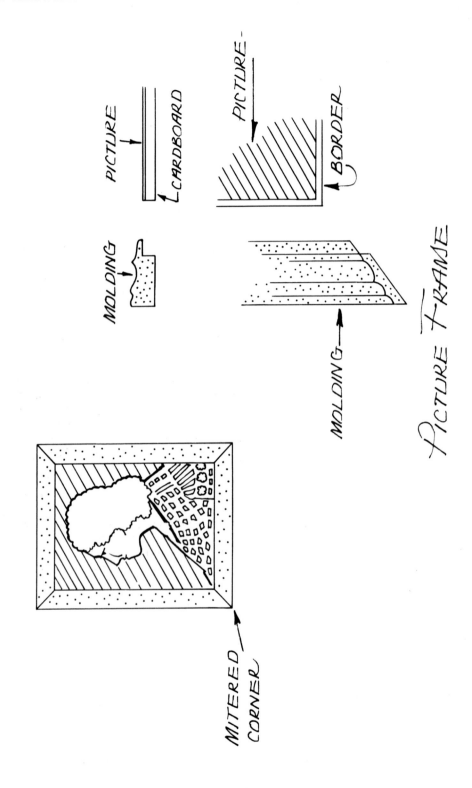

PICTURE

CARDBOARD

MOLDING

PICTURE

BORDER

MOLDING

MITERED CORNER

PICTURE FRAME

PICTURE FRAMES

Big, old-fashioned belt buckles, often with open metalwork edges (they were popular in the forties) can simply be touched up with gold paint if they are metal. If they are cloth-covered, strip off the material and paint the buckle gold. Remove the prong with your Dremel Moto-Tool or with tin snips and plenty of elbow grease.

Some jewelry findings frame silhouettes nicely—for example, the oval ring that holds a locket picture in place.

To make an elaborate picture frame, glue together Popsicle sticks and paste découpage filigree on the frame surface with Elmer's glue. Tone down its brightness a little with yellow ochre.

Balsa frames take stain well and can be grooved easily with an emery board.

Strips of veneer make striking frames. Now that miniature making has become so popular you can buy picture frame molding in miniature. Pamela White of Boston, Massachusetts, makes her frames from this molding.

PAMELA WHITE'S FRAME

1. Purchase Northeast Scale Model molding. It comes in many styles and sizes. Stain, paint, or gild at least 10 inches of the molding.

2. Mount your picture on cardboard $1/16$ inch thick or less. Leave a $1/16$-inch border on both picture and cardboard. This will be hidden when the picture is framed.

3. With your miter box or mat knife, gently cut the molding to fit around the picture, making 45-degree angles for four mitred corners. The thin "lip" side of the molding should be sloping in toward the picture when you are done, and the inside measurement of the molding should be the size of the picture you want to have show, not the size of the cardboard mount.

4. Cut and glue the molding with a good white glue, fitting the thin lip of the frame over the cardboard one side at a time, joining the molding precisely and closely. There will be several triangles of lip to discard because of the mitered corners.

5. Touch up any exposed wood with paint, stain, or gilt.

SHELLS AND BUTTERFLIES

If you're a nature lover, try framing tiny shells or mini-butterflies the way Dee Snyder of North Palm Beach, Florida, does. Her shells are collected on Florida beaches; her butterflies are snippets of bright color cut from magazines and glued into butterfly shapes on an attractive backing.

Mini-butterflies, also fashioned by Dee Snyder, begin with snippets of colored pictures from magazines.

BOOKS

If there are pictures in your dollhouse or miniature setting, surely you'll want books, too. The simplest kind of book—the kind that stays in a bookcase simply to provide color and atmosphere—can be cut from balsa or basswood. Glue fabric or leather a little larger than the block of wood over the wood to make the cover. Glove leather is the perfect weight if wood is used underneath it—there must be one old glove without a mate around your house somewhere. To simulate page edges, rub the top, bottom, and side of the block pages lightly with Treasure Gold wax.

A more bookish-looking book is made from high quality typing paper cut into strips. Lit Lapsley of Richmond, Virginia, devised this system for preparing a dollhouse quickie:

LIT LAPSLEY'S BOOK

1. Cut four strips of paper about 2 inches long and 1 inch wide. Put the strips one on top of the other and fold them in two. Write what you wish on them with a fine-point pen; you will have sixteen pages or one "signature."

2. Cut four more strips, stack and fold them, and continue your writing. Now you

Balsa wood is the material Elspeth uses for little books.

Homespun makes a decorative cover for some of the books that Lit Lapsley of Richmond, Virginia, designs.

have two signatures and a thirty-two-page book. Make two or three more signatures in the same way, always being sure to fold them before writing on them.

3. Label the spine of each signature with small dots so you are sure that the signatures stay in order—one small dot for the first signature; two for the second, et cetera.

4. Now make four bigger dots, evenly spaced, along the spine of each signature.

5. Hold all the folded signatures together (a snap type clothespin is useful for this purpose). Cut a rectangle of thin white cloth backing slightly less than 2 by 1 inches so it is a little smaller than the signatures. Fold it around the outside of the batch of signatures.

6. Use polyester thread for fine fabrics. You will use this to sew through the large dots you have made in the spines of the signatures and through the gauze. Starting on the outside, sew through the gauze and the large dots up the back of one signature, down the back of the next, up the third, down the fourth. Be sure, when you are finished, that your needle and thread are on the outside of the book. Make a small knot. (Be careful during this sewing to keep the signatures close together so they won't gape, but not so close that they pull at the spine.) This is the way a real book is sewn.

7. Run Elmer's glue down the spine of the book. With two little boards (strips of basswood will do) to protect the book, clamp it into a vise to dry, making sure that the pages are all even. Let it dry overnight. This gluing reinforces the sewing.

8. In the morning, cut a piece of old leather a little bigger than the open book. Apply glue to the white cloth (it will seep through to the back page) and glue the leather to this paper-cloth combination on the front and back, but not to the spine. Again, let the book dry between boards clamped in a vise.

9. To decorate the cover, cut letters or a title from a book or magazine and glue it to the leather.

FLOWERS AND FLOWER POTS

Since any house looks better with plants and flowers here and there, hold onto old toothpaste caps. They're useful for all sorts of things in a miniature household—lamp shades, wastepaper baskets—but above all, with a few touches of paint they're perfect flower pots. Transistor parts or milk and jelly containers from restaurants fill the bill too. Or use quilling paper, coiling a strip of it tightly, then pushing the bottom out and spreading the inside with Elmer's glue so the pot keeps its shape. Let this pot dry before proceeding.

To prepare the flower pot for flowers, squirt it full of silicone glue and fill it with craft sand. Star macaroni, colored as you choose and affixed to pins or wire, make pretty flowers, with some plastic leaves cut to appropriate size for greenery.

B.H.

DRIED FLOWERS

You may also dry real small flowers, of course. Susan Sirkis uses a mixture of one half Borax and one half cornstarch. Gently place little field flowers in this mixture, stems down, in a container that has an airtight cover. Carefully cover the flowers with more of the mixture. Cover the container and store in a cool, dry place for a few weeks. You can also dry flowers in fine white or yellow sand as Audrey Steiner Bugbee describes in *How to Dry Flowers the Easy Way*. For this method, leave the container open; tiny flowers will be dry in three to five days.

"SILK" FLOWERS

With some artistry, you can make rosebuds in miniature out of ribbon (they will look like a small version of Thai silk flowers). Folding and sewing narrow ribbon around fine green tie wire is the basic method for doing this.

BEAD FLOWERS

Here are Susan Sirkis' directions:

1. Cut four 1½-inch lengths of beading wire. String four seed beads on each wire and twist the ends of the wire together. These will be the petals.

2. Loop a 1½-inch piece of wire through a small yellow bead and twist the four petals around that bead, securing with wire and leaving enough wire to make a stem. Make the leaves by stringing five green beads on a wire and twisting them around the wire stem. Wrap the stem with florist's green tape.

METAL FLOWERS

Some of the prettiest miniature flowers are made from the thin metal used to seal wine bottles. Smooth the metal with the back of a spoon. Cut it into petals. Glue the petals together and to a tie wire stem (crafts shops carry them for beading) with Duco household cement or quick epoxy. Paint them with matte acrylic paint or Flo-Paque. This is another Susan Sirkis design.

Sculpey is another material from which flowers can be fashioned if you are artistic. But if you use it, before drying or painting, be sure to make a hole with a toothpick where you will insert your stem. Then, when the flower is dry and painted, slip in a wire wrapped in florist's green tape.

GARDEN HOSE

If you plan to grow miniature flowers outdoors, you should have a hose to put in a garage or leave in the garden. Make it of green vinyl tubing and transistor connectors. Twist the transistors into the tubing to make nozzles.

Candlesticks, vases, trays, candy dishes, salt and
pepper shakers—all can be made with a handful of
findings and beads by an imaginative craftsman.
(Peter Schaaf for Mini Mundus)

DISPLAY DOMES

The glass domes that come from trinket machines or the ampules at the end of an orchid corsage make glass domes for displaying miniature seashells, straw flowers, or other treasures. If you use an ampule, you'll probably have to go to your local hardware store to have the glass cut. (Through miniature-making, you get acquainted with many people!) Glue the shells, or the straw flower arrangement, or a tiny sculpture made in Sculpey to a button the size of the base of the dome. Then put glue around the edge of the button and fit the dome over it.

WASTEBASKETS

Large-size toothpaste caps or thimbles make attractive wastepaper baskets. So does tubing covered with pretty mini-wallpaper and rick-rack. Cut the bottom from cardboard. Just remember that, like the rest of your setting, your wastepaper basket should be in the inch-to-the-foot scale.

The cans that contain 35 mm. film make trash cans, if you decorate them with silver paint and draw in vertical stripes.

KNITTING

Mini-knitting, placed on a chair where an inhabitant of your setting has left it, is done on straight pins and isn't easy. (At Mini Mundus, one of the shops where mini-knitting is sold, one delighted customer, a woman lawyer, came back six weeks after she first saw the store's knitting on pins. Her fingers were covered with Band-Aids, but she proudly showed off her two rows of straight-pin knitting.) Use mending yarn or three-ply yarn taken apart for this.

PAPERWEIGHTS

On the subject of buttons, look among your old ones for a pretty glass one that would make a nice mini-paperweight.

Mini-knitting on straight pins is effective but hard on the fingertips. (Peter Schaaf for Mini Mundus)

JIGSAW PUZZLES

Find a mini-picture in a magazine. (You will need two copies of the magazine so you can glue one copy to the cover of the box you make for the puzzle.) Glue the puzzle to thin cardboard (¹/₃₂-inch, or an index card) and cut into jigsaw swirls.

FISH TANK

A little fish tank is an easy accessory to make. Simply cut down a plastic toothbrush container—the kind with square corners. Paint the edges green with acrylic paint. Cut the fish for the tank from bright plastic flowers. Put sand in the tank bottom and stick the fish on pins stuck into the sand. Hide the pins with seaweed made from the leaves of plastic flowers. Or you can simply glue the fish to the inside of the tank.

COAT HANGERS

Bend them from florist's wire.

CARPET BEATER

Make a hole in one end of a small dowel and insert a 16-gauge wire, twisted to the proper shape, into it.

ASHTRAYS

Tiny buttons or seashells make fine ashtrays.

A miniature fish tank can be made from a toothbrush container. Beads painted gold and glued onto common pins with the heads cut off become a picture frame when B. Jean Silva sets to work. The matting at the corners is heavy foil from a hobby shop. An index card, painted, cut down to mini-size, and glued to a thin piece of glove leather becomes a blotter. At the corners of the blotter is black plastic tape from the five-and-ten. The inkwell is a jewelry finding.

A granny afghan by Agnes Miri goes especially well with the bed that her father, Joseph Maiorano of Ridgewood, New Jersey, makes of ⅛-inch brass rods, ⅛-inch brass ferrules, and solder.

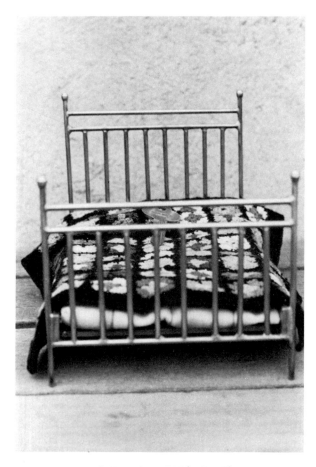

CHAPTER 5

A teddy bear looks well on a dollhouse bed. (*Peter Schaaf for Mini Mundus*)

SOFT GOODS

Many a devotee has been lured into miniature-making by way of soft goods. Needlepointers are challenged by the idea of what some miniature-makers call petit petit point, where the scale is 40 stitches to the inch, used for samplers and upholstery and done on a silk gauze backing. And whoever heard of an Aubusson carpet no bigger than a sheet of typewriter paper? But if you have good eyesight and nimble fingers, there's no reason why you can't make an in-scale rug with 20 stitches to the inch, or a miniature granny afghan or a ribbon quilt.

If fine needlework is not your area of expertise, however, there are ways of approximating soft goods for your room setting. The right dishcloth, for example, can become a woven coverlet for a bed and a crocheted pot holder will make a rug.

Penelope or mono needlepoint canvas is the base for Nancy Hebner's 20-stitches-to-the-inch needlepoint Oriental. (See design graph, p. 39.)

RUGS

IMITATION ORIENTAL RUG

1. Find an Oriental rug design that you like in a book. Copy it in pencil onto the right side of a piece of velveteen. Do not cut the material yet.

2. Draw over the penciled design with felt-tip pens in various colors. Cut the material, leaving a ⅓-inch border to be fringed.

3. Paint the back with Elmer's glue.

GENUINE ORIENTAL RUG

Nancy Hebner of Carmel, New York, comes naturally by her affection for Orientals, for her father was a dealer in them. The accompanying miniature design was reduced from a rug that is on her living room floor.

Materials

Penelope or mono needlepoint canvas that will give you 20 stitches to the inch

One strand of Persian Paternayan brand wool available by the skein or ounce at yarn stores

A No. 17, 18 or 19 needlepoint needle. It should thread easily, but not distort the canvas while you are stitching.

1. Cut the canvas 12 by 10 inches. Bind the edges with masking tape.

2. Find the center of the canvas by creasing it in half first by the length and then by the width so it is in quarters. Mark the center with an indelible marker. From this center point, count the number of stitches on the graph to determine where the outside borders will be. If you wish, you may then mark all designs onto the canvas with a marker or follow the design graph as you work. In either case, start the rug by working the outside borders first, then the corner designs. Working from the center, complete the medallion design. Finish by filling in the background. Use the half cross stitch instead of the continental, to avoid bulkiness.

3. When you have finished your rug, it will probably be crooked. To straighten it, you must block it. You will need a piece of wood larger than the rug, covered with brown paper. With a dampened cloth and hot iron, steam the back of the rug. You will now find you can straighten it by pulling. Using rust-proof push pins, pin the damp rug to the board, keeping it straight. Pin along the unworked canvas. (Never put pins through finished work). Let it dry completely and remove from board.

4. To bind the edges of your rug, use 2-inch-wide bias seam binding in a color as

An American Colonial braided rug can be made of crochet cotton. Barbara Taylor Hackney designed this one.

close to the outside border as you can find. Open the folded edge and pin it to the right side of the rug, easing the tape around the corners. Turn the work to the wrong side and sew the binding as close as possible to the last row of needlepoint. Trim away excess canvas and turn the tape to the back. Work with your fingers to flatten. Sew the binding to the back of the rug with a slip stitch and miter the corners.

AMERICAN COLONIAL BRAIDED RUG

A braided rug of colors that coordinate with your room setting will always go well in an eighteenth-century room. Here are how-to-do-it directions from Barbara Taylor Hackney, a New York magazine artist who doesn't have time and energy to make a full-scale braided rug so is making mini-rugs instead.

Materials
Coats & Clark's Speed Cro-Sheen mercerized cotton in three colors
A roll of two-inch masking tape
A needle and thread

1. Cut crochet cotton in approximately 4-foot lengths. Braid together one strand of each color into a tricolor braid. Make a solid color braid of the darkest color. Stitch the ends together so they will not become unbraided and ravel. Braid approximately three times as much of the tri-color as of the solid color.

2. Lay out strips of the masking tape, overlapping them until you have a slightly larger surface than the size of the rug planned. Starting with the tricolor braid, lay out the braid on the sticky side. Continue round and round, alternating tricolor with solid color as desired. Be sure braids are placed very close together, but not overlapping. Also, do not allow the braid to turn over at any time.

3. As you lay the braid on the tape, you are seeing the underside of the rug. Be sure when you come to an end that it stays on the underside of the rug, facing you. When the desired size is reached, trim the excess tape close to the rug shape.

4. Now stitch the braids together with tiny stitches, starting at the center and working round and round to the outside. Pick up only a small bit of the braid strands as you stitch to ensure that no stitches show on the right side of the rug. Trim excess frayed parts.

5. Remove the tape carefully. At this point, the rug will look caplike and out of shape. With a steam iron, press it flat. A little spray starch applied to the underside of the rug before pressing will help to keep the rug flat and very slightly stiff.

HOOKED RUGS

Hooked rugs are also charming in miniature settings. Fenner Wheeler of West Mystic, Connecticut, works with a punch needle used for punch embroidery, very fine darning or Shetland wool, and #12 Penelope needlepoint canvas to make a traditional log cabin rug. You can also hook with a small metal crochet hook instead of a punch. But unless you make a dowel handle for the hook, it will be hard to work with. For a frame to keep the material taut while you work, use an embroidery hoop.

1. A workable size would be 4¼ by 5¼ inches (including border). Divide the canvas into squares. Each square and the outside border of the rug will be outlined in black. Hook these parts first.

2. As you work, hold 8 to 12 inches of yarn underneath the backing onto which you have sketched the squares. Poke the hook down through the mesh and pull up a loop of wool ⅛ inch high. Repeat this from mesh to mesh (or every other mesh to every other mesh, depending on how dense you want the rug to be).

3. Do two or three rows with one color; then cut the last loop of that color after you have pulled it through. It should be cut at exactly the same height as the other loops.

4. When one block is done with the loops all running in one direction, do the loops in the next block all running in another direction: i.e., if the first square was a horizontal one, the next one should be vertical.

5. When the hooking of the whole rug is done, trim the canvas close to the border and whip the edge with dark thread to keep the rug from raveling. To be really safe, apply Elmer's glue thinly with a brush on the wrong side. Let it dry awhile and then lay a piece of wax paper over the back. Weight it down with something heavy enough to flatten it. Let the rug dry completely. It should lie flat.

SKIN RUGS

Of course you can have animal skin rugs, too—either genuine or imitation. When your fur goes to the furrier for remodeling, ask for the scraps and cut them into bearskin shapes or whatever you like. A skin rug that is a whole tiny animal skin came with a dollhouse that *Miniature Gazette* editor Robert von Fliss bought, though he has yet to identify the kind of rodent it came from!

LOG CABIN HOOKED RUG

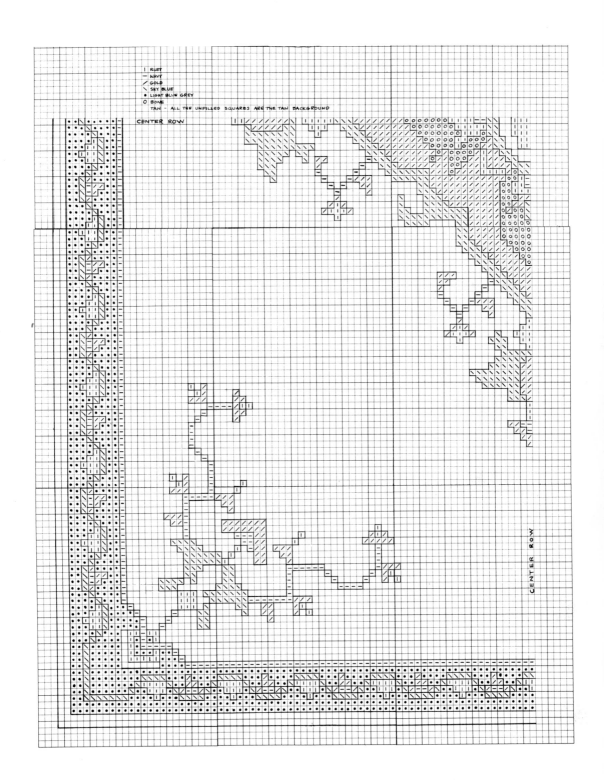

I RUST
— NAVY
/ GOLD
\ SKY BLUE
• LIGHT BLUE GREY
O BONE
TAN — ALL THE UNFILLED SQUARES ARE THE TAN BACKGROUND

CENTER ROW

CENTER ROW

Cross-stitch samplers—postage stamp size (or a wee bit bigger)—will brighten the walls of your miniature setting. (Peter Schaaf for Mini Mundus)

AFGHANS AND QUILTS

A long time ago, years before the current enthusiasm for miniatures hit the nation, Elizabeth Fisher of Middletown, Connecticut, was making miniature objects and writing how-to books about them. Here are her instructions for a miniature granny afghan.

GRANNY AFGHAN

1. For a granny afghan, use a single strand of six-strand embroidery cotton. Decide what color combinations you wish to use and choose accordingly. You will also need a No. 14 crochet hook.

2. Chain six, fasten closed, chain three. Count that chain as one double crochet and put two more double crochets in the circle you have just made.

3. Chain one, three double crochet, chain one, three inside double crochet until you have four bunches of three double crochet, then chain one and join.

4. Change the color of the thread, attach at chain one, chain three, and two more double crochet in the chain one space.

5. Chain one and put three more double crochet in the same chain one space, chain one and three double crochet, chain one, three double crochet in the same space, and continue until you have six double crochet and one chain in each chain space.

6. Chain one of your background color. Attach it at a chain one space and at the corners of the little square you already have*, put three double crochet, chain one, three double crochet*, chain one, three double crochet on the side where the chain one space is. Now you are at another corner. Repeat from * to * for each corner.

7. Sew the squares together. The afghan should be four or five squares wide and six or seven long. By keeping the chain ones in line, you can make an elegant afghan. Finish it with fringe.

8. To make the fringe, cut a sturdy piece of cardboard 1½ inches long by about 1 inch wide. Use the full six strands of embroidery cotton for each piece of fringe and wind it smoothly around the cardboard. Cut the thread along one side of the cardboard for uniform fringe length.

9. To attach the fringe, put your hook at the center of the strip of embroidery cotton and pull it through the edge of the square. Leave the loop and pull the ends through the loop. Then pull up tight and keep going all around the afghan. Trim to a length that will please you. Each section of fringe should have 12 pieces in it.

RIBBON QUILT

Ribbons can be used to create a patchwork effect in miniature quilts and pillows with a lot less work than individual patches. The directions below are by Judy Faulkner of Ho-Ho-Kus, New Jersey, and are for a double bed quilt using ¾-inch velvet ribbon. Variations will be considered after step-by-step directions.

The overall size of the quilt will be 7¼ by 6½ inches, plus lace. The overall pillow size (make two) is 2 by 1½ inches plus lace.

Materials

2½ yards each of two colors (A and B) of ½-inch velvet ribbon

1½ yards of ⅜-inch lace

An 8 by 12-inch piece of unbleached muslin or similar fabric

An 8 by 12-inch piece of fabric of a complementary color to be the reverse side of the finished quilt

Embroidery floss in a color complementary to the ribbon colors.

1. Cut a piece of the muslin 8 by 7¼ inches.

2. Cut nine 8-inch strips of Color A.

3. Lay strips out on muslin, covering it from side to side but leaving a ⅜-inch margin at the top and the bottom. Baste the strips down on one side ⅜ inch from the edge.

4. Cut eleven 7¼ inch strips of Color B.

5. Weave Color B strips through Color A thus: Push the first strip firmly against the row of basting. Anchor each strip with a pin at the beginning and end after the weaving is completed.

6. After all the strips have been woven in, baste around the remaining three sides, ⅜ inch from the edge.

7. Several types of decorative embroidery are possible. You can make a French knot at each square corner. You can make a cross-stitch at each square corner. Do a blanket stitch around the outer edge of the quilt.

8. Baste lace around the quilt. The outer edge of the lace should be toward the center of the quilt. The inner edge of the lace should overlap the basting line a bit. Gather the lace at the corners. Fold gathers so that only the edge of the lace gets caught in the seam you will make to join quilt to decorative backing.

9. Cut the decorative backing the same size as the muslin.

10. Pin and baste it to the quilt with the right sides together.

11. Machine- or hand-stitch around all four sides, ⅜ inch from the edge, leaving a 2½-inch opening for turning.

12. Clip the corners; turn and press quilt. Remove any visible basting. Slip-stitch the opening.

Pillows

1. Cut four 3-inch strips of Color A and six 2¼-inch strips of Color B.

2. Lay strips of A down on the remaining muslin in two groups of two. Baste one edge of each group ⅜ inch from the end of the ribbon.

3. Weave in and baste Color B as in quilt. Trim muslin down to the size of the ribbon rectangles.

4. Do decorative stitching as you did in the quilt.

5. Attach lace as you did to the quilt. Be especially careful to keep folds of gathered lace out of the seam of a small piece.

6. Cut two pieces of decorative backing the same size as the pillows. Attach the backing as you did with the quilt. Clip, turn, and press.

7. Stuff each pillow with cotton.

8. Slip-stitch opening.

Variations

1. Not all beds will look well with a rectangular quilt. If you have an opening in a footboard or headboard, you might like to shape a quilt that looks more like a three- or four-limbed cross. If that is the case, strips of A and B colors will each have to be of a different size from the one in the directions; the muslin backing should be cut the same size as the desired overall size of the finished quilt with a ⅜-inch seam allowance added on all sides. Ribbon strips have a ⅜-inch seam allowance at *each* end.

Finally, be inventive. Use a bit of by-guess-and-by-gosh in determining yardages. Throw in a few strips of another ribbon to create a plaid effect. Substitute a bit of lace for some of the ribbon strips. Elaborate on simple decorative embroidery.

The Tree of Life pattern in miniature is done in crewel embroidery by Mrs. Roderick Lewin of Ashburnham, Massachusetts. (Concord Depot)

HANDKERCHIEF CURTAINS

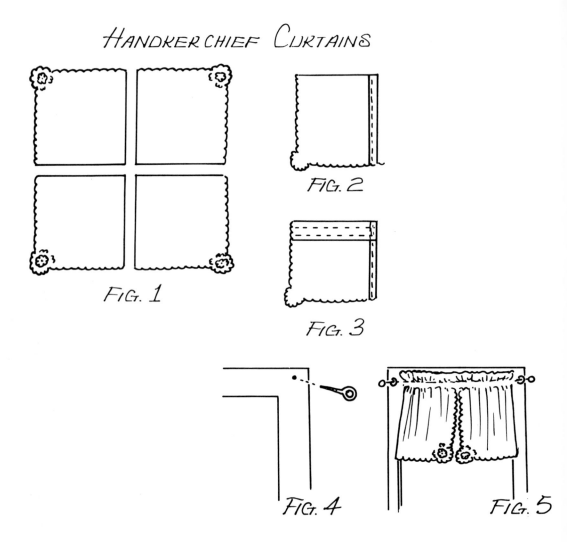

FIG. 1

FIG. 2

FIG. 3

FIG. 4

FIG. 5

CURTAINS

Scraps of old lace curtains make exquisite curtains for a formal dining room, but dime store handkerchiefs can be prettily hung at a window, too. Gretchen Deans of New Canaan, Connecticut, offers these instructions for handkerchief café curtains.

HANDKERCHIEF CURTAINS

Materials
A fancy handkerchief
A needle and thread
A $^1/_{16}$-inch wooden dowel to hang curtains on. (You can also use Q-Tips or round wooden strips bought at a hobby shop and cut with a single-edge razor blade to the exact length of the window frame.)
Screw-eyes or staples cut in half for brackets.

1. Cut the handkerchief into four equal squares (fig. 1).
2. Make a ¼-inch hem on inside of each square. Hem ⅜ inch on the other raw edge of the square. Stitch again about ¼ inch down through ⅜-inch row of stitching, leaving enough fabric at the top for a ruffle (figs. 2 and 3).
3. Screw screw-eyes into the window frame, or hammer in staples (fig. 4).
4. Insert the rod through the hem of the curtain where the double stitching is, and place the rod in brackets by the sides of the window (fig. 5). With glue, attach pretty beads to the ends of the rods, if you wish— but remember, if you do, the curtains cannot be removed for laundering.

Since curtains that hang in a miniature setting are likely to go limp after a while, brush a solution of half Elmer's glue and half water over the backs of the curtains; then form them into folds and let them dry. Bear in mind, however, that curtains treated in this way may discolor after some months. Another method is to put the dowel with the curtains on it on a cork board, hold it in place with two tacks under the ends of the dowel, pull the curtain down and pin it into folds. Then spray with unscented hair spray. Let it set for several hours to dry before you unpin and hang the curtain. Test both methods on fabric scraps first.

GLASS CURTAINS

Material from a good slip, blouse, or scarf will make fine glass curtains as long as it is not too bulky. But don't use satin. If your window is 2 inches wide, each curtain should be 2½ inches wide. The length should be that of the window. Use a selvage for one edge of the curtain. Blind-stitch the top where you will insert the rod. Make a ⅛-inch hem at the bottom. Try to hem without turning under double if you can, for turning under will make your curtains bulky. (Incidentally, miniaturists who don't like to sew can avoid hemming with thread by hemming with white glue instead.)

DRAPERIES

Use lightweight double-knit fabric for draperies. Make very tiny box pleats in the top. Draperies can be either slightly longer than the window or floor-length. Make tieback tassels of draper's cording. Split one big tassel, using the threads of only one strand for a miniature tassel. Cut it into 2-inch lengths.

Clay's Choice is the pattern of this quilt sewn by New Jerseyite Marti Dinkel. (Concord Depot)

This gay patchwork is the handiwork of thirteen-year-old Jessica Elfenbein of New Milford, New Jersey.

Twenty-four stitches to the inch were used by Mitzi
Van Horn of Richmond, Virginia, for this delicate
petit point rug. Her petit point also decorates the
chair. (Mitzi Van Horn)

It looks like metal but it isn't—a sewing machine designed largely from filigree by Claire Danos of Ridgewood, New Jersey.

CHAPTER 6

Mitzi Van Horn creates these eighteenth-century lanterns.

MAKE IT FROM METAL

Until you stop to think about it, you never realize how many objects in a house are made from metal. And if you do think about it, you are likely to dismiss metal miniatures as impossible, unless you happen to be a blacksmith, which few of us are.

But in the miniature world, things are not always what they seem—metallic paint can transform cardboard into flatware or plumber's sweat caps into cooking pots. And even real metal miniatures aren't hard to make, according to Al Atkins of Carmel, New York, who *is* a blacksmith. With the equipment listed below, and the miniature-maker's eye that sees something small in almost everything, you should be able to supply yourself with pie plates, weathervanes, locks, buckets, hinges, doorknobs, toleware, and dozens of other objects.

To get started, you'll find that you can do most of your work with these tools:

A good pair of tin snips to cut lightweight metal

A jeweler's anvil

A ¹/₁₆-inch welding rod

An eggbeater drill

Sandpaper

Rubber cement, epoxy, spray paint

Hammer

Vise

This collection of kitchen utensils (including a skimmer made from a jeweler's dome-shaped screen) were fashioned by blacksmith Al Atkins of Carmel, New York—but anyone can make them, he says.

C-clamps
Propane torch
Soldering iron, solder, and flux
Unimat with attachment for metal-
   working
Dremel Moto-Tool
Pliers

KITCHENWARE

TRAY

To make a fine toleware tray, pry off the lid of a Colman's mustard can, a cocoa can, or any old-fashioned spice can. Spray-paint it with black enamel and decorate it with Testor's paint.

BAKING TINS

You probably never noticed it before, but a pry-off bottle cap is a perfectly shaped fluted pie tin. Remove the printing with steel wool.

Cut rectangles from TV dinner pans to make cookie sheets.

This striking stone fireplace that Rob Lyon builds provides an attractive background for many metal accessories. (Richard Benjamin)

SKIMMER

Make a skimmer from a jeweler's round dome-shaped screen. If you want a brass handle, glue on a $1/16$-inch brazing rod with 5-minute clear epoxy. To make a steel handle, use a $1/16$-inch steel welding rod. Both are available at welders' supply shops.

CUTLERY

One dexterous miniature-maker cuts tiny grooves into slivers of wood to make handles. Then he breaks stainless steel razor blades into knife and cleaver shapes by hitting them with a hammer or a rock. The blades are slipped into the pre-cut grooves. Obviously this is a somewhat haphazard approach—you may have to break several blades before you get the right shapes.

An easier and much safer method for making blades is to cut a piece of flattened tin can into the shapes you want with tin snips. You can also hammer a straight pin flat to make a knife. Glue it with epoxy to a piece of round toothpick cut to the length of a handle.

POTS AND PANS

Check your local gumball machine for one that has a souvenir frying pan. Play it until you win. If you want a cast-iron pan, spray your prize with flat black paint. If you prefer copper, use Testor's copper paint.

This cleaver was made by Rob Lyon from a razor blade and the "pewter" mugs from .22 shells.

Good copper pots take a bit more work, but when you think what the real ones cost, it's certainly worth it. Your pots will be made from the copper sweat caps that are used with copper tubing, with coat hanger wire for the handles. Since the sweat caps come in a wide variety of sizes, you can make all kinds of copper pieces, including a double boiler and even a lobster pot. The instructions below also show how to make a copper kettle.

1. The sweat cap is the body of the pot.

2. To make the handle, snip off a piece of coat hanger the length of the diameter of the pot with your wire cutter or pliers and heat it with a propane torch until it is cherry-red. Leave the wire round for most of its length, but pound the very end flat where you will attach it to the pot. With a pair of pliers, bend the flat piece so that it is at right angles to the rest of the handle.

3. Sandpaper the spot on the pot where the handle will be attached—and sandpaper the handle where it will be attached, too. (You must sandpaper both parts or the glue will not stick.) Glue the handle to the pot with epoxy.

4. If you prefer a kettle, drill holes with a hand drill on both sides of the pot and slip and hook a piece of wire through. Be sure the gauge you choose goes with the size of the pot. Paint the handle black and spray the pot with clear lacquer.

COAL SCUTTLE

In a country kitchen, a coal scuttle would be a useful item. Make yours from the coffee cream container you get in a restaurant. Make a hole on both sides of the creamer, and loop No. 10 wire through. Don't forget that a coal scuttle has a big loop. Spray the scuttle with flat black enamel.

Nylon curtain and coat hanger wire are the materials Nancy Hebner uses to make a fireplace screen.

MUG

The shell from a .22, cut to appropriate size with a jeweler's saw, becomes a pewter mug. Make the handle from a thin piece of brass, or a piece of wire. Glue it on with epoxy.

FLATIRON

Make an iron from balsa wood and spray-paint it silver. Bend a paper clip into a staple shape for the handle.

FIREPLACE ACCESSORIES

SCREENS

To fashion a fireplace screen, cut and bend a piece of copper wire that is about the thickness of picture wire into three pieces. The center piece should be the width of your fireplace and designed with a slight decorative "hill" in the center of the top. The two side pieces should be rectangular, the same height as the lowest part of the center section. (See your own fireplace screen for the exact design.) In depth, the side pieces should be as deep as your hearth. Glue these pieces with epoxy onto a nylon curtain, and when the epoxy is dry, cut out the three parts of the screen, cutting as close as possible to the outside of the wire edging. Then sew the sections of the screen together with black thread. Spray with black paint.

A simpler but less authentic-looking fireplace screen can be made from an old wire hair roller. Unroll it and cut it down to the right size.

You can also make fireplace screens from copper or aluminum window screening. Bend it tight around 16- or 18-gauge copper wire with your needle-nose pliers. Glue it with Duco.

Copper screening and 16-gauge copper wire are combined in B. Jean Silva's fireplace screen. The little kettle to hang over the hearth once was the top of an old-fashioned copper salt shaker.

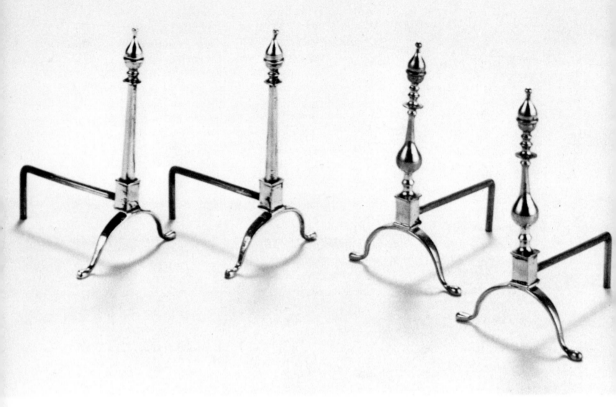

These elegant andirons were cast by Donald Butt-field, who makes his miniatures in New Jersey. (Photography Unlimited)

ANDIRONS

Al Atkins offers these directions for making a pair of andirons from two large sardine can keys and two pieces of lightweight coat hanger.

1. With your tin snips, snip the key off just at the end of the split.

2. Pull the sides of the split apart with your pliers. Heat them with a propane torch to help you to bend the legs to a standing shape without breaking them.

3. To form the rails for each andiron, cut and bend pieces of coat hanger, flattening and doing the bending with the aid of a propane torch. The front end of each rail should bend up slightly where it will be glued to the key. The back end should be bent down to a right angle to form a foot.

4. Sand both the hanger and the key

where they will be glued together. Glue them with epoxy.

5. When the glue has dried, snip the handle off each key and in its place glue a metal bead, a BB, or a small ball bearing. Again, use epoxy for the gluing.

6. Paint the andirons with flat black spray paint.

Elspeth, a designer of miniature patterns from Bethesda, Maryland, makes andirons by

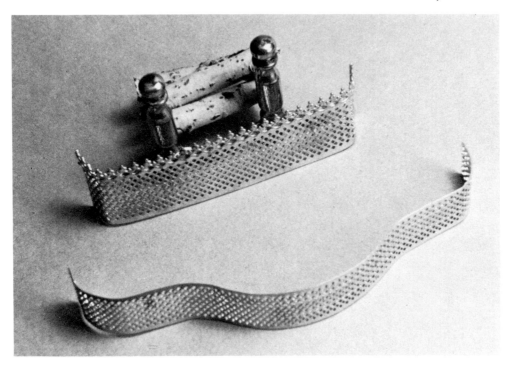

Jeweler's brass gallery can be turned into a fine fireplace fender like this one by Pamela White.

arranging beads of various sizes along a corsage pin. Remove the head. Make the rail from mat board. Paint it black and glue it to the head assembly with epoxy. Paint the beads with gesso and when they are dry, gild them.

You can make simple andirons from steel cut nails. For the back foot piece you will need half a nail. To break it, clamp it in a vise and hit it crossways with a hammer (steel nails are very hard).

FENDER

A pretty piece of stiff metallic paper or a decorative strip of jeweler's brass gallery will make a fine fireplace fender.

TONGS AND SHOVEL

Elspeth also uses beads assembled on wire to make her fireplace tongs and shovels. The wire is painted black, the beads gold. The "shovel" is cut from a card, folded, glued to the wire handle, and then painted black.

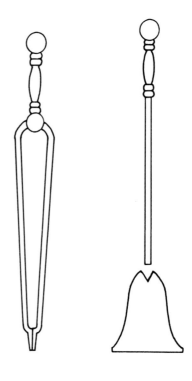

After a rainstorm, an Al Atkins umbrella drips beside a cane in an umbrella stand that was one of those lucky finds miniaturists make. Mr. Atkins isn't sure what it is or where he found it, but it's just the right size for his umbrellas.

UMBRELLA

There really ought to be an umbrella or two in the hallway of your miniature setting.

1. Using a compass, draw a circle with a 2-inch radius on a piece of white paper. Draw lines to make eight pie-shaped pieces, but don't cut them. Do snip off the outside ends of the pieces to make an octagon, however. Using the accompanying pattern, cut a piece of black, unshiny lining material.

2. Make the stem for the umbrella out of a single strand of bell wire with insulation on it. You can buy this at a hardware or electronics equipment store.

3. Bend the wire to make a handle crook, then ring the wire around with a knife and remove the covering everywhere except the handle.

4. Poke the umbrella stem through the fabric at the center of the circle so that a tiny tip—about ¼ inch long—shows through on the other side.

5. Using Elmer's and a toothpick to dab it on, glue the stem to the fabric from the center to the outside edge.

6. Now make ribs of printer's staple wire, available from a bindery, or from straightened strands of picture wire. Cut seven of these 2⅛ inches long (so they stick out a bit from the perimeter). Glue them, evenly spaced, onto the fabric octagon. Let them dry. Then fold each section around the handle. If any of the ribs are too long, snip them off. Twist the umbrella as tight as you can.

7. Wrap heavy-duty black thread around and around the umbrella and knot the thread to hold the umbrella closed, or loop it over a tiny button. If you like, glue an appropriate jewelry finding to the tip of the umbrella.

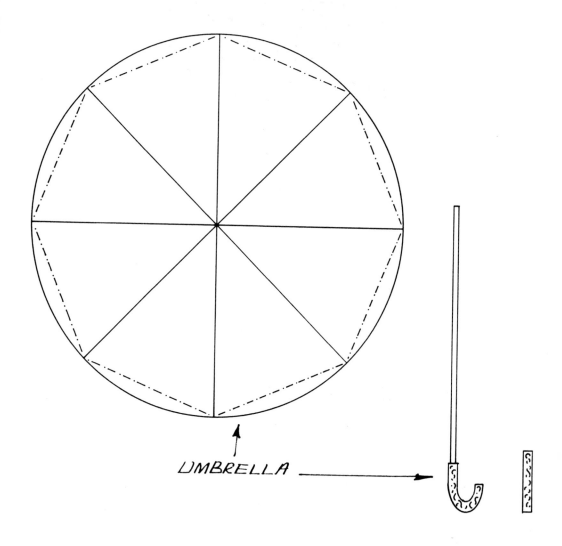

UMBRELLA

ODDS AND ENDS

A small Band-Aid box, painted white, makes a perfect clothes hamper.

Twist wire into a pair of eyeglass frames and with the flat edge of a nail polish brush, spread clear nail polish across the frames where the glass should be. The polish should form a bubble and catch. Or simply drop a dab of Elmer's glue into the hole instead. It will dry clear, believe it or not!

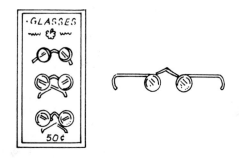

WHALE WEATHERVANE

A flattened tin can or a piece of shim brass or copper sheeting from a hobby shop is the basis for this piece. If you use a can, run it through your can opener, removing the top and the bottom. The best cans from which to fashion miniature metal objects are those that are coated with genuine tin—most food cans and solvent cans are in this category. Beverage cans are not. After you remove the top and bottom from the can, cut it open with your tin snips and straighten it out. Beware of sharp edges when working with cans. Cans with paper labels instead of printing on the can itself work best. If there is printing, however, it can be removed with semicoarse steel wool.

1. When the can has been flattened, spread rubber cement on it and on a tracing of the accompanying pattern. Let each side get almost dry before you glue one to the other. Then cut the whale shape out of the metal with tin snips. Peel off the pattern and spray-paint the whale black.

2. As you see, there is a small appendage left at the bottom of the whale. This will make the tube into which the weathervane staff will be inserted. To form it into a tubular shape, cut small notches on both sides where it is attached to the whale. Then roll it into a tube form and insert a small rod cut from a coat hanger.

3. Drill a small hole in the roof of your house, and insert the weathervane.

DOORKNOBS AND HINGES

Brass tacks with rounded tops or brass escutcheon pins for nailing brass plates on doors are perfectly satisfactory as doorknobs. If your Dremel Moto-Tool has a steel saw attachment it will easily cut the end of the brass escutcheon pin to the right length.

Hinges can simply be cut from black leather, but if you actually make them of metal, it calls for some handiwork. Here is the way Larry Garnett of Richmond, Virginia, makes them:

1. Cut the metal (again, use tin-plated steel cans) into the two shapes called for in the pattern. Make sure that they are of a size proportionate to your door.

2. Use a small file to make a very neat fit of the tongue of one piece into the slot in the other piece.

3. With your long round-nosed pliers, bend the long ends of each side of the hinge.

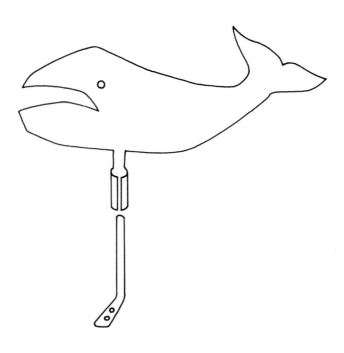

(These long ends that fit around the hinge pin are called gudgeons.) You will have to do this very carefully with the tip end of your pliers. Roll up tight, all the way back to the base of the hinge.

4. Slide the two halves of the hinge together, fitting the rolled edges together to make one long roll. Then push a small straight pin all the way down through the three holes and cut off any excess pin at the bottom. File-cut the end of the pin to remove the sharp edge.

5. Punch two $1/32$-inch holes in each side of the hinge. Use a jeweler's sharp metal punch for this or drill with a No. 60 or a $1/16$-inch drill. In using your drill or punch, go from the side away from the wood toward the wood on which the hinge will be installed. Straighten out any bends this may have caused. (A punch is preferable to a drill here, for the little burrs that the punch leaves are helpful when you attach the hinge.)

6. Use epoxy or Duco cement to attach the hinges to the doors, but make sure no glue gets onto the pin. After applying glue to the wood and metal surfaces, let both dry slightly before joining them. Put a small amount of glue on the end of the pin to keep it from coming out.

HORSESHOE

Would you like a horseshoe to hang and bring good fortune to your miniature household!

Cut a small piece of coat hanger with a wire cutter or pliers and bend it to a tight horseshoe shape. (It must be tight now because it will open later.) Using a propane torch and a hammer, beat the piece of hanger to $1/32$-inch flatness. If you have a vise with an anvil this will facilitate matters, and small jewelers' anvils are not expensive. If you have no anvil, clasp a hammer, head up, in your vise, and being very careful of your fingers, hold the piece of hanger on it and beat it flat with another hammer. File the ends for finishing.

A master miniaturist of Richmond, Virginia, Mitzi Van Horn, makes this eighteenth-century brass rim lock and key.

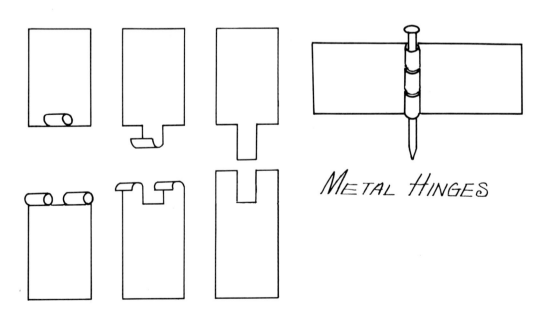

METAL HINGES

B. Jean Silva finds belt buckles of the right shape exceptional as turkey platters. A thimble becomes an ice bucket (crystal beads are the ice). Polyform and a bottle cap combine to make a cherry pie. Jewelry findings are the salt and pepper shakers and napkin rings are chain links.

CHAPTER 7

Beads are the mints and jewelry findings the candle-sticks and vase in this just-before-teatime assortment of miniature objects. (Peter Schaaf for Mini Mundus)

No guests at a miniaturist's table will ever go hungry. The food is certain to be plentiful and elegantly offered. There will be silver serving dishes and the china will probably be Delft. To start with, of course, you need table linen.

TABLECLOTHS

A thin white handkerchief, a scrap of gingham with a small design, or a piece of lace, depending on the formality of the occasion, will make an attractive tablecloth. To keep it from sliding off the table, hold it in place with a round tab of the wax sold in candle stores for keeping candles steady.

A long, draped Victorian cloth looks well on a round table. If the cloth hangs low, sweeping, or nearly sweeping, the floor, whip-stitch very fine wire (a radio supply store will have it) around the bottom of the cloth on the inside. Cup your hand over the cloth as you lay it on the table, bending the wire into folds.

SETTING AN ELEGANT TABLE

A sliced red eraser is the bologna on Barbara Taylor Hackney's luncheon table, and a gum eraser is the loaf of bread. Jewelry findings are also important in this setting. (J. Kender)

PLACE MATS

PAPER

To make paper place mats, simply decorate rectangles of paper with felt-tipped colored pens. The jump rings that jewelers use to hold two beads together make nice napkin rings.

CLOTH (SEWN)

You can make cloth place mats from long strips of a fine material like gingham. Run the material through your sewing machine, out-lining rectangles a little more than 1½ inches wide by ¾ inch deep with the smallest stitch on your machine. When the rectangles are outlined, cut them apart, close to the border but not through the stitches. The matching napkins should be of the thinnest material you can find.

CLOTH (FRINGED)

If you don't want to bother with stitching, simply take small scraps of thin material with a small design from your sewing basket, cut them into rectangles, and fringe the edges.

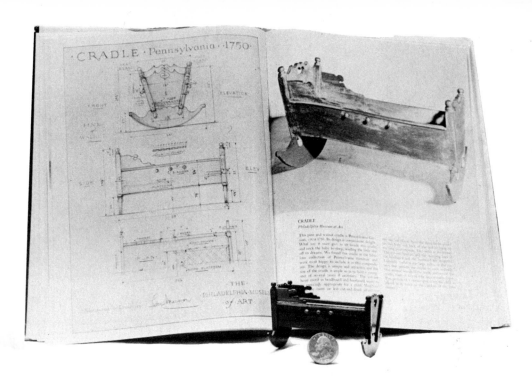

F. L. Patterson III of Newcastle, Delaware, reduces the plans for full-size antiques from books on furniture to construct cradles like this one.

❧ A Colonial "keeping room," the center of the early American home, is one of the simplest miniature settings to furnish, and if you have never made furniture before, it is a good place to start. You need only a handful of pieces—a trestle table and a few benches, some slat-back chairs, perhaps a hutch to display the fine crockery that you've made, and a sea chest filled with your linens. Many of the pieces can be made with just an X-acto knife, or a mat knife, files and emery board, a small drill and a small saw, a triangle, a miter box, a ruler, and glue. Though a keeping room is especially suited for these items, and directions for making one follow, the furniture can be used in virtually any kind of room setting.

Mrs. Raymond H. Crouch of Croton-on-Hudson, New York, offers this design for her keeping room.

FURNITURE

KEEPING ROOM

You will need to do all work on floor and sides and do all finishing touches before gluing and nailing this room together.

This Colonial keeping room with its monumental fireplace, Welsh dresser, and corner cupboard was executed by Jane and Raymond Crouch of Croton-on-Hudson, New York. (Alice M. Leighner)

FLOOR

1. To make the floor, you will need a 22-inch-wide by 14-inch-deep piece of ¼-inch plywood.

2. To put on top of this, stain random widths and lengths of basswood, for instance, 1 by ¹/₃₂-inch, ½ by ¹/₃₂-inch, and ¾ by ¹/₃₂-inch. Minwax is a good stain, either Early American or Colonial Maple finish. Put it on with a cloth, and when the desired shade is achieved, wipe off the excess. Staining must be done before gluing, for glue will seal the wood and keep the stain from penetrating.

3. Glue pieces onto floorboard with Duco cement. When laying floorboards, mark parallel lines on the plywood floor every couple of inches to keep the floorboards themselves parallel. If you don't do this, they will tend to go off somewhat at an angle. With a tiny nail, make simulated nail holes in the four corners.

4. When floors are laid, wax them.

SIDES

1. For the sides (walls) of your room, you will need two pieces of plywood, 14 inches wide by 9 inches high. The window should be cut on the left side, 2½ inches in from the front. If you want a door, put one in 2½ inches in from the back of the room, but a door is not necessary.

BACK

1. The back piece should be 21½ inches wide by 9 inches high.

PLASTERING

1. With sides and back flat, put on Spackle to simulate plastered walls. (It can be roughly smoothed on with fingers.) When it is completely dry, paint it white.

FIREPLACE

1. From ¼-inch plywood, with a hobby saw cut one 9 by 10-inch piece to be the front of the fireplace and one 9 by 2¼-inch piece to be the side of the fireplace. (There is no need for another side, for it will abut the side wall.) In larger piece, cut fireplace opening 5 inches high. Cut so that 1⅜ inches remains on one side of the opening, 2 inches on the other.

2. Glue the 9 by 2¼-inch side of the fireplace at right angles to the back of the room, attaching with Elmer's glue or Duco cement.

3. Glue one end of the front of the fireplace to the side piece you have just glued and the other end to the side wall of the room.

4. From small scraps of wood, cut strips to form the inside arch of the fireplace, using the smallest strips for the inside of the curve. Glue with Elmer's. These can be rough pieces, for they will be Spackled. If you like, cut an oven door for the front 1¼ inches wide by a little more than 1 inch deep from ⅛-inch basswood. Cut and bend a piece of food can metal for a latch. Glue it on with epoxy. Paint the door flat black and glue to fireplace 3 inches from bottom.

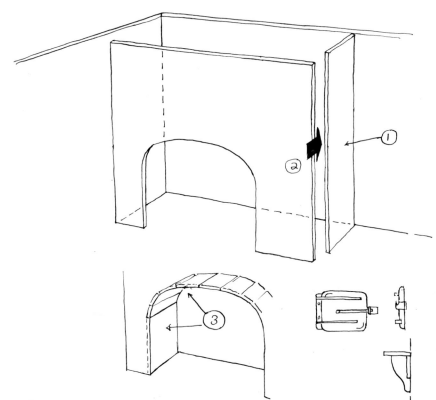

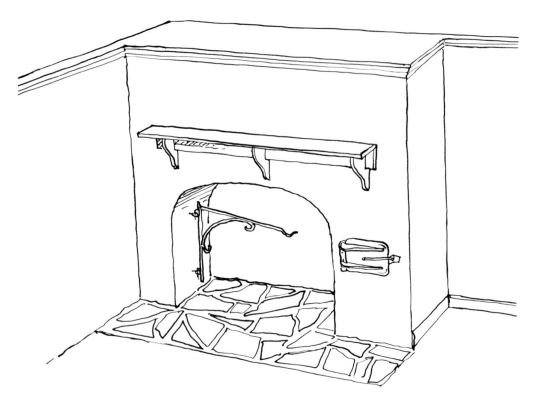

5. Cut an 8-inch-long mantel shelf from ¾-inch white pine or basswood. Cut three bracket-like supports and glue to the ends and middle of the shelf. Let dry, then apply glue to the backs of the supports and the shelf and glue shelf in place 2½ inches from top of room.

6. Cover the outside of the fireplace with a thin coat of Spackle, but do not plaster the inside after you have glued it in position, for it will shrink and crack if you do. Paint the fireplace white. Blacken the inside with paint if you like.

7. For the hearth, apply Spackle. Cut thin pieces of sandstone if available, and lay them in the Spackle. If not, use any thin, flat stones for a stone hearth.

FINISHING TOUCHES

1. Window: the inside of the window should be trimmed with strips of wood ¼ by ¹/₃₂-inch, stained as you wish, and glued in place with Elmer's. Around the outer edges of the window, glue stained strips ⅜ by ¹/₃₂-inch. There is no need to miter the corners, however you must butt them. For the window ledge, glue a ⅜-inch-long piece of ¹/₁₆-inch basswood at bottom of window opening.

2. Baseboards: around the bottom of the room pieces, glue ⅜-inch strips of ¹/₁₆-inch basswood. At the top of this baseboard, round off with a file, so there is a slight slope toward the front.

3. Glue the room together.

4. When the room is dry, glue ceiling molding flush with the top edge. Make it by gluing strips of wood together cut in lengths to fit the sides and the back, up to the fireplace, of the room. Begin with a ½ by ¹/₃₂-inch piece. Glue onto this, flush with the top edge, a ¼ by ¹/₃₂-inch piece, and on top of it a ³/₃₂ quarter round piece. Top this with a ½ by ¹/₃₂-inch piece glued at right angles to the rest of the molding. The molding will have to be mitered at the corner. After molding is in place, to simulate main supports of room, glue ¼ by ¼-inch square strips in right-hand back corner and at front edges.

5. To cover up the cut of the plywood on the front edge of the floor, glue a ¼ by ¹/₃₂-inch stained strip. On the sides, do the same.

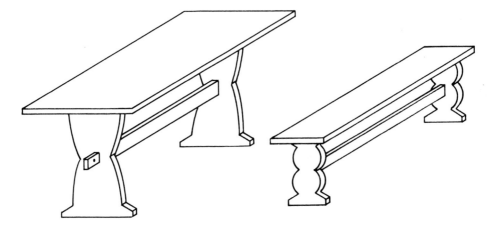

The easiest furniture to begin with is a trestle table and benches. These directions come from Fran Cook of La Mirada, California, who also designed the Welsh dresser, corner cupboard, Colonial child's hearth chair, and Early American water bench (where buckets were kept) that follow.

TENON TRESTLE TABLE AND BENCHES

Materials
White glue
⅛-inch basswood or pine for table top
¹/₃₂-inch basswood or pine for legs, stretchers, and benches
Oil stain
Toothpicks

ASSEMBLY

1. With hobby saw, cut out the accompanying parts (p. 78).
2. Sand and bevel edges of table top, bench tops, table stretchers, and sides of legs. Do not sand top or bottom of legs, smooth only their sides and side edges.
3. Stain all pieces with a good oil stain. It is essential to do your staining before you begin to assemble. Once you apply glue, the stain will not take.
4. Cut a square hole in each of two table legs to receive tenon of lower stretcher.

These should be a snug fit, not so loose as to be sloppy and not so tight as to split the leg. Trim tenons with a small knife until they fit.

5. Put a small amount of glue on each tenon, and a small dab inside each hole to receive the tenon. Push through until tight against each leg. While glue is still wet, turn this assembly upside down on a piece of aluminum foil.
6. Now apply a small dab of glue to each end of the upper stretcher, place it in position between the 2 legs, centered properly, and even with the tops of the legs (fig. 1). Check to see legs are square and put a rubber band around this assembly.
7. Before glue dries, wipe off excess with a damp rag, and touch up the stain.
8. When dry, drill a small hole in each tenon, just where it protrudes beyond the table leg. Carefully fit the toothpick piece or a ¼-inch piece of ¹/₁₆-inch dowel through each hole and glue it in place (fig. 2).
9. When these are dry, turn the table top upside down, and put a small line of glue along the top of each leg and the top of the upper stretcher. Place this in the bottom of the table top, center it carefully, press it firmly, rubbing back and forth a few times to insure a good fit (fig. 3).
10. Repeat the same procedure for the benches, but remember the rungs have no through tenons as the table stretcher does.

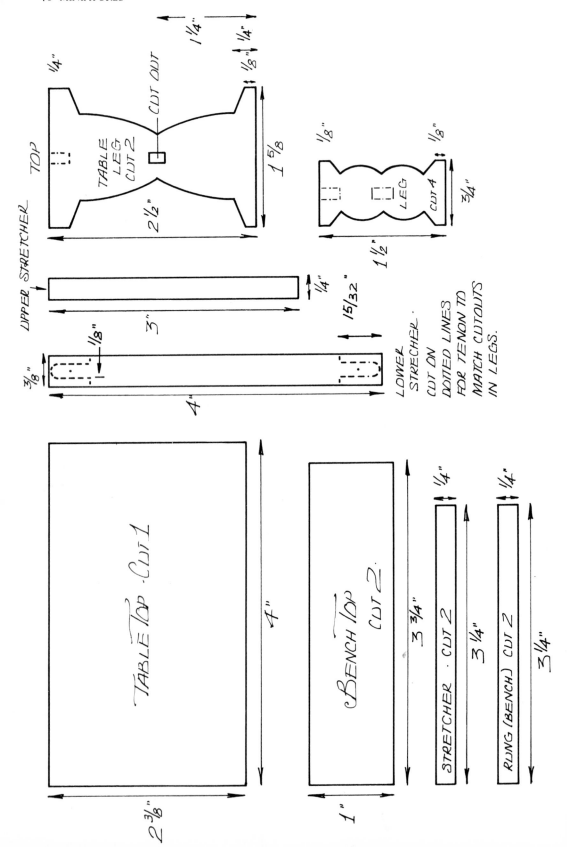

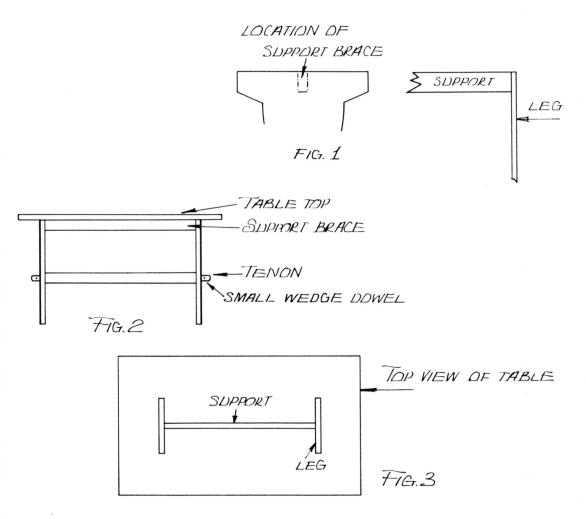

LOCATION OF SUPPORT BRACE

FIG. 1

SUPPORT

LEG

TABLE TOP

SUPPORT BRACE

TENON

SMALL WEDGE DOWEL

FIG. 2

TOP VIEW OF TABLE

SUPPORT

LEG

FIG. 3

TENON TRESTLE TABLE ASSEMBLY

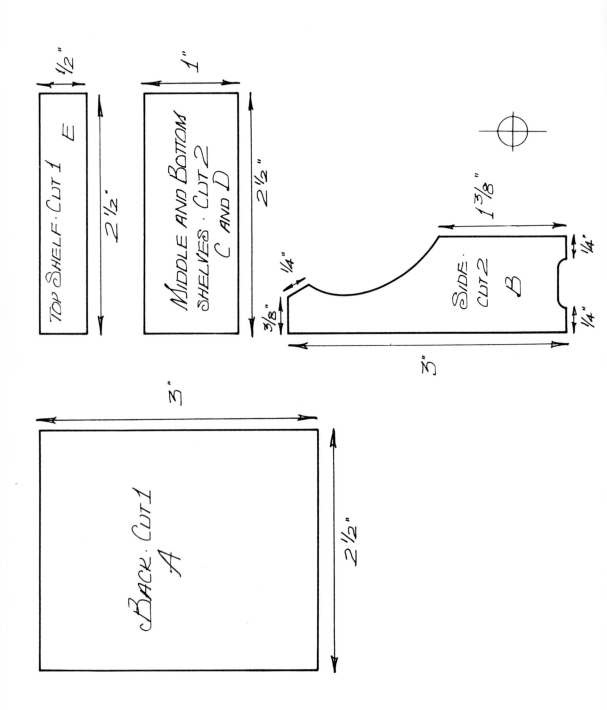

Top Shelf · Cut 1 — E — ½" × 2½"

Middle and Bottom Shelves · Cut 2 — C and D — 1" × 2½"

Side · Cut 2 — B — 3" × 1³⁄₈" — 3/8" — ¼" — ¼" — ¼"

Back · Cut 1 — A — 3" × 2½"

EARLY AMERICAN WATER BENCH

Materials
White glue
Stain
$^3/_{32}$-inch bass or pine

1. Cut pieces from accompanying pattern.
2. Gently smooth—don't round—the edges of the back piece with sandpaper.
3. Sand and round all front edges of the sides and shelves.
4. Stain all pieces.
5. Then assemble the water bench by placing a thin line of glue on the side edges of the back (A). Lay the back flat on a worksheet of aluminum foil. Gently press the side pieces (B) into place against the back. Allow them to dry.
6. Draw a line $^1/_{32}$-inch from the bottom of the sides and back. Glue the side and back edges of the lowest shelf (C) into place at this location. The rounded edge, of course, should be kept to the front.
7. Glue the second shelf (D) into place 1 inch above shelf C.
8. Set the smallest shelf (E) into place in the same manner 1¼ inches above D. Note that shelf E should fit where the arrow is and should not be flush with the top.

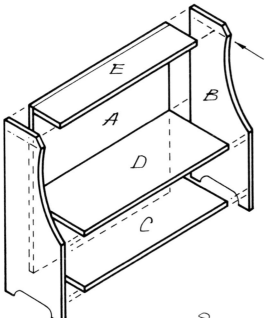

Shelf E should fit where arrow shows; it should not be flush with the top.

Water Bench Assembly

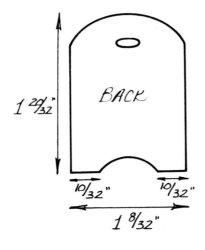

1 29/32"

BACK

10/32" 10/32"

1 8/32"

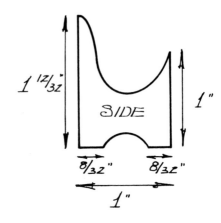

1 12/32"

SIDE

1"

8/32" 8/32"

1"

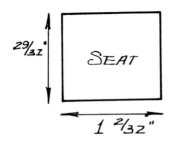

29/32"

SEAT

1 2/32"

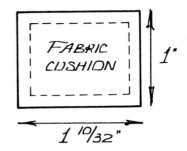

FABRIC CUSHION

1"

1 10/32"

COLONIAL CHILD'S HEARTH CHAIR

Materials
White glue
Stain
$3/32$-inch bass or pine
Material for cushion and cotton to fill it

1. Cut pieces from accompanying pattern.

2. Sand and smooth the curved top edge of the back, the leg piece, and the hand grip near the top.

3. Sand and smooth the curved arm piece and the leg cut-out. Smooth the side edges of the back slightly.

4. Lightly smooth the sides and the back of the seat. The front edge should be rounded.

5. Stain the pieces now. If you would prefer to paint them, wait until you have finished the chair.

6. Using a piece of aluminum foil as a worksheet, lay the back piece flat. Then run a thin line of glue along the back edges of the

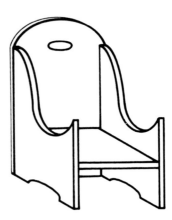

side pieces, setting them in place on top of the back. Allow them to dry.

7. Measure ⅜ inch from the bottom edges of the sides and back piece. Make a light mark. Apply glue to the sides and back edges of the seat and set it into place where you have made the mark.

8. While the chair is drying, make your cushion from the pattern and stuff it, not too full, with cotton.

Use ceramics, Sculpey, or Polyform figurines, and cardboard or plastic painted to resemble pewter to decorate a Welsh dresser like this handmade one by William B. Wright from the collection of Cookie Ziemba of New City, New York.

WELSH DRESSER

Materials

$^3/_{32}$-inch bass or pine
2 pairs of hinges and brads
4 3-mm white beads and sequin pins
White glue
Toothpicks
Stain

BASE ASSEMBLY

1. Cut out dresser base pieces from the accompanying pattern.

2. Sand all pieces of the base, A—M and DB–1—DB–4, except for the base top (H). The sides and front edges of this piece are lightly rounded. Stain all pieces of the base.

3. Run a thin line of glue along the side edges of the back (B), i.e., the 2½-inch edges. Lay the piece flat on a foil worksheet to do this. Butt the 2½-inch sides of pieces (A) to the glue along the sides of (B), being careful to line up the tops of these pieces; otherwise your dresser top will not fit (fig. 1, p. 87).

4. Before the glue dries on this assembly, apply a thin line of glue to both ends of strip (C) and place it even with the top edges of sides (A) and the back (B) (fig. 1). Hold together with a rubber band until dry.

5. Apply glue to the front edge of shelf (E) and set face strip (D) in place on its front edge (fig. 2).

6. Apply a thin line of glue along the sides and back edges of shelf (E) and set it in place ½ inch below (C); repeat with shelf (F) and the front kickplate (G) as shown in figure 3. Make sure the kickplate is flush with the bottom of the cabinet.

7. After applying glue to the top of the base back (B), sides (A), and strip (C), lay cabinet flat on its back on foil and set the top piece (H) in place, flush against the back. Be sure that the overhang is equal on both sides. The front edge will extend over the base, but there will be no overhang at the back.

8. Glue the kickplate facing (M) on the front of (G), making certain the edges line up properly.

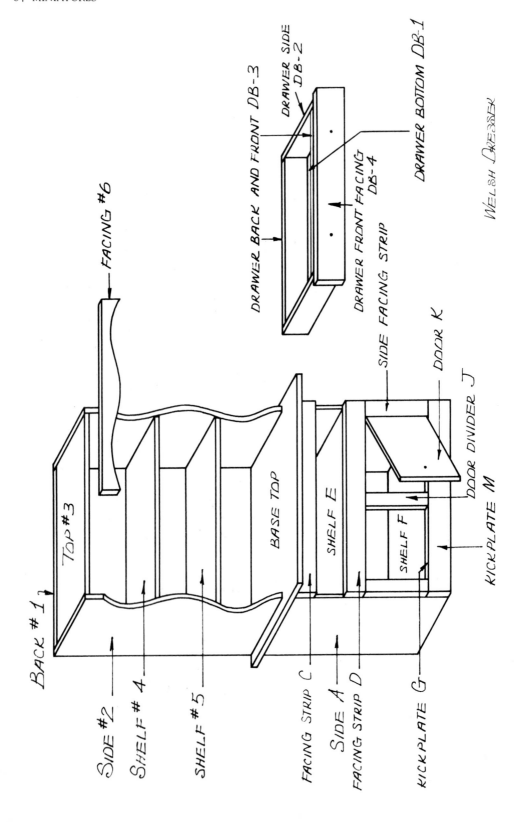

DRAWER SIDE DB-2

DRAWER BACK AND FRONT DB-3

DRAWER FRONT FACING DB-4

DRAWER BOTTOM DB-1

FACING #6

SIDE FACING STRIP

DOOR K

DOOR DIVIDER J

WELSH DRESSER

BACK #1

TOP #3

BASE TOP

SHELF E

SHELF F

KICKPLATE M

SIDE #2

SHELF #4

SHELF #5

FACING STRIP C

SIDE A

FACING STRIP D

KICKPLATE G

Welsh Dresser · Server Base

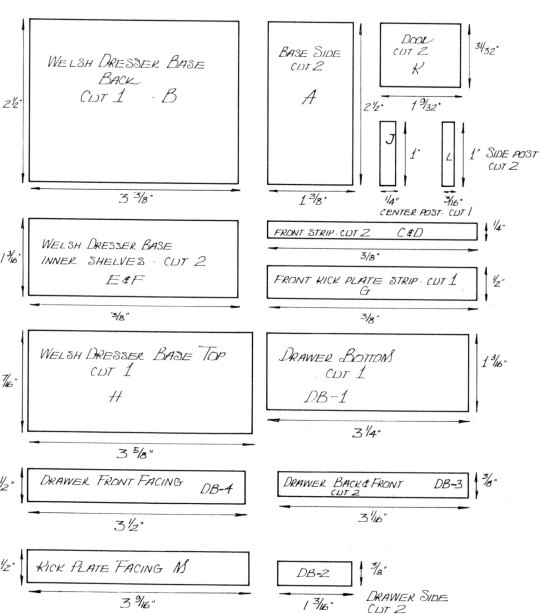

WELSH DRESSER BASE
BACK
CUT 1 · B
2½"
3 ³/₈"

BASE SIDE
CUT 2
A
2½"
1 ³/₈"

Door
CUT 2
K
3 ¹¹/₃₂"
1 ⁹/₃₂"

J
¼"
L
1"
1" SIDE POST
CUT 2
³/₁₆"
CENTER POST · CUT 1

WELSH DRESSER BASE
INNER SHELVES · CUT 2
E & F
1 ³/₁₆"
³/₈"

FRONT STRIP · CUT 2   C & D
¼"
³/₈"

FRONT KICK PLATE STRIP · CUT 1
G
½"
³/₈"

WELSH DRESSER BASE TOP
CUT 1
H
⁷/₁₆"
3 ⁵/₈"

DRAWER BOTTOMS
CUT 1
DB-1
1 ³/₁₆"
3 ¼"

DRAWER FRONT FACING   DB-4
½"
3 ½"

DRAWER BACK & FRONT   DB-3
CUT 2
³/₈"
3 ¹/₁₆"

KICK PLATE FACING M
½"
3 ⁹/₁₆"

DB-2
1 ³/₁₆"
³/₈"
DRAWER SIDE
CUT 2

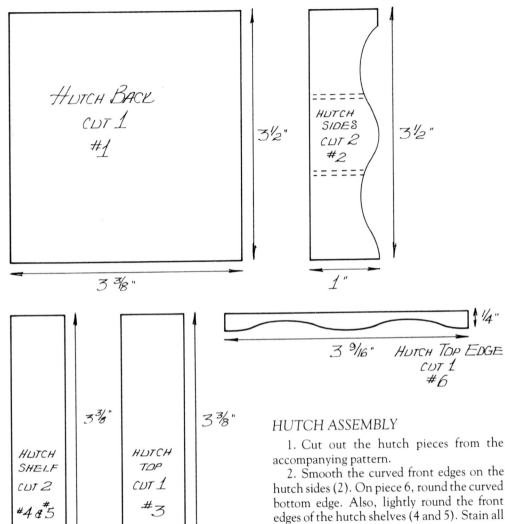

HUTCH BACK
CUT 1
#1

3½"

3 ⅜"

HUTCH SIDES
CUT 2
#2

3½"

1"

¼"

3 9/16"   HUTCH TOP EDGE
CUT 1
#6

HUTCH SHELF
CUT 2
#4 & 5

3 ⅜"

25/32"

HUTCH TOP
CUT 1
#3

3 ⅜"

29/32"

HUTCH ASSEMBLY

1. Cut out the hutch pieces from the accompanying pattern.

2. Smooth the curved front edges on the hutch sides (2). On piece 6, round the curved bottom edge. Also, lightly round the front edges of the hutch shelves (4 and 5). Stain all pieces before assembly.

3. Lay the hutch back (1) on a foil worksheet. Run a thin line of glue along the 3½-inch sides. Butt sides of piece (2) into place along the glued edges. Match the top and the bottom for evenness. (fig. 4)

4. Now glue the hutch top (3) into place, as in figure 5, being certain that all the edges are even at the top. Hold tight with rubber bands until dry.

5. On the inside of the hutch, measure down 1¹/₁₆ inches from the top and make a mark at this level on both sides, and at either end of the back. This mark is where shelf (4) is to be glued. Repeat, but 2⅛ inches from the top, for shelf (5). In each case, it is the tops of the shelves that should be placed along these lines.

WELSH DRESSER ASSEMBLY

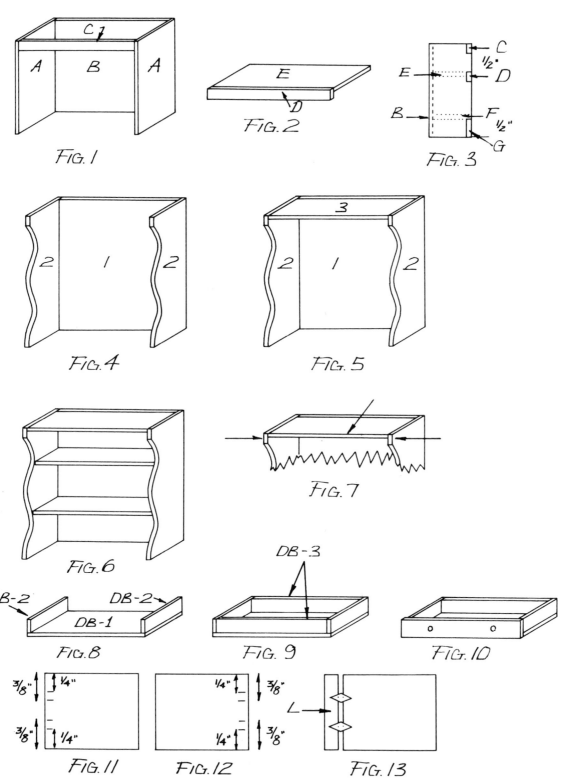

FIG. 1

FIG. 2

FIG. 3

FIG. 4

FIG. 5

FIG. 6

FIG. 7

FIG. 8

FIG. 9

FIG. 10

FIG. 11

FIG. 12

FIG. 13

A hutch can also be made with a patterned background for your miniature china.

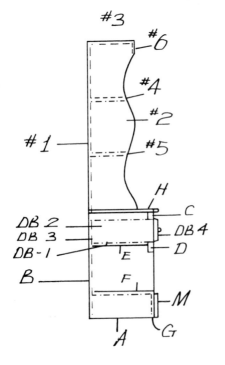

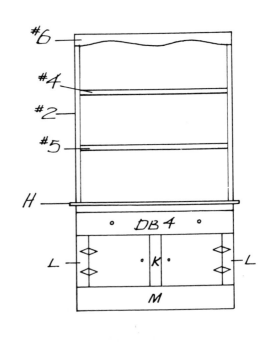

6. Apply a thin line of glue along the sides and back edges of hutch shelves (4 and 5). Set these into place (fig. 6), and allow them to dry. Make sure they line up carefully with witness marks before the glue dries.

7. Put a thin line of glue along edges where it is indicated by the arrows in figure 7. Set the top edge of (6) into place flush with the top edge. When the hutch unit is dry, apply glue to the bottom edges and center the hutch on the base.

DRAWER ASSEMBLY

1. Lay the drawer bottom (DB-1) on the foil. Apply glue to the bottom edges of the drawer sides (DB-2) and put them in place on top of (DB-1), as in figure 8.

2. To glue the drawer front and back in place (fig. 9), apply glue to their ends and bottom edges. After placing them between the drawer sides, make sure they're flush front and back.

3. When the drawer is dry, fit it into the drawer slot. If any trimming is required, do it now with sandpaper or a fine knife.

4. Coat the drawer front (DB-3) with glue, and apply the drawer facing (DB-4). Center it so it overhangs evenly on both sides. Use small sequin pins and white beads to simulate porcelain knobs. When placing the knobs, space them about ¾ inch from the edge of the drawer (fig. 10).

DOOR ASSEMBLY

1. Place side post (L) on your foil. Lay a door beside it (fig. 13). Leave a small space between the two to allow for easy door opening. Put a strap hinge on top and mark ¼ inch and ⅜ inch from the top and the same from the bottom (fig. 11). Fit your hinge between these two marks. Using a pin pushed through each hole in the hinges, make a mark in the wood below.

2. Place a dab of glue on the back of the hinges. Push brads through the holes in the hinges, then on through the marks in the wood. Use a brad pusher or fine pliers. Repeat with all hinge brads. Allow to dry. Clip the excess as close to the underside as possible. The finished door should look as in fig. 13. Repeat for right-hand door.

3. Apply glue to both the ends and backside of L. Set in place against the side of the base (fig. 12).

4. When the doors are in place, there will be a good-sized gap between them. Don't despair. This is where (J) is glued to fill the gap. But be sure to leave enough leeway so the doors will open easily.

CORNER CUPBOARD

Materials
White glue
³/₃₂-inch bass or pine
Hinges and brads
3-mm porcelain type beads
Sequin pins
Stain

1. Transfer the pattern to the wood and cut out all pieces with your jigsaw.

2. Make 45-degree miter cuts on the front and back edges of the cupboard sides (A), as in figure 1 (p. 91).

3. Mark the inside faces of the cupboard sides (A) where the dotted lines show on the pattern. This will make it easier to see where to insert the shelves later (fig. 2). Round the curved edge of the top facing (E).

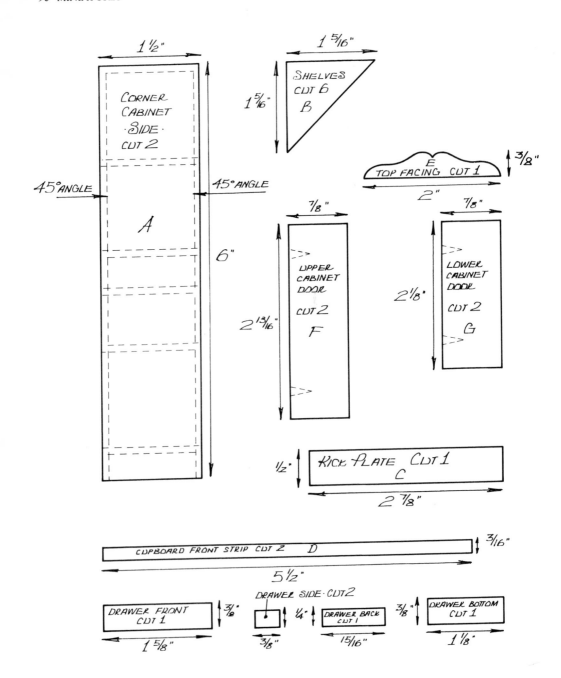

FIG. 1

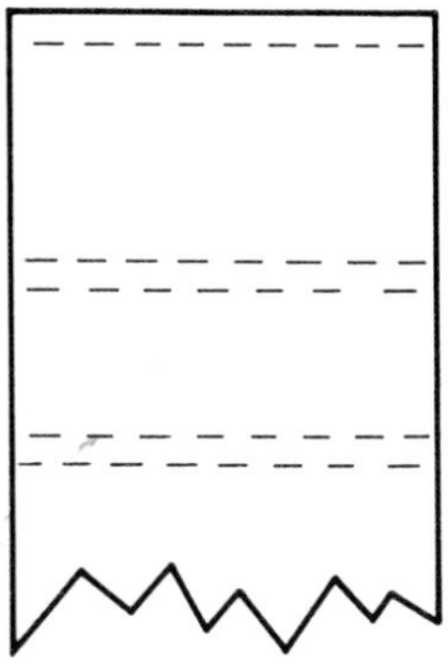

FIG. 2

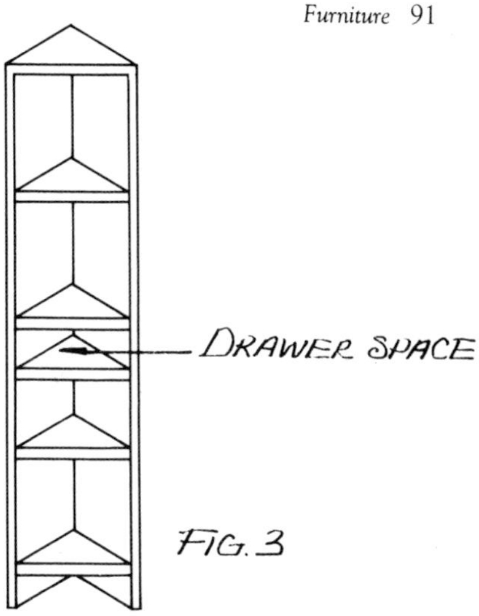

FIG. 3

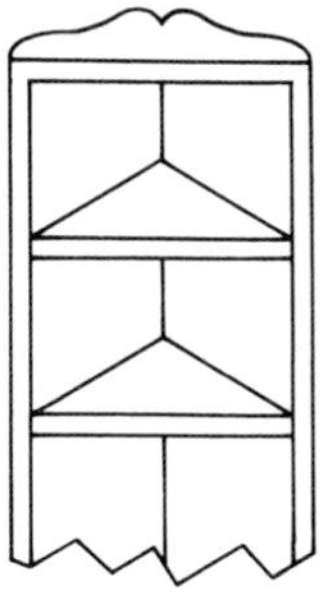

DRAWER SPACE

FIG. 4

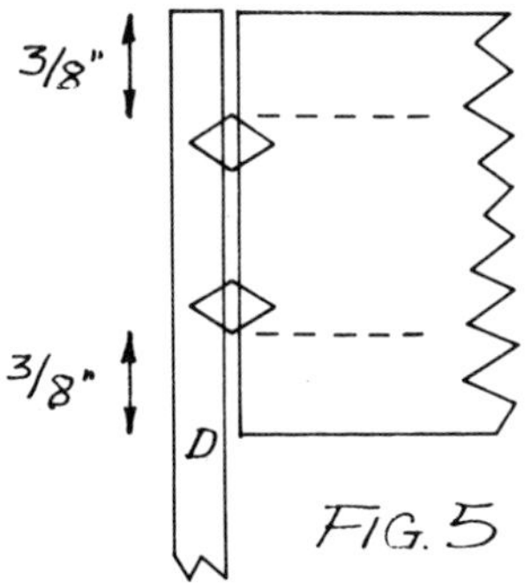

3/8"

3/8"

D

FIG. 5

F.

G.

D →

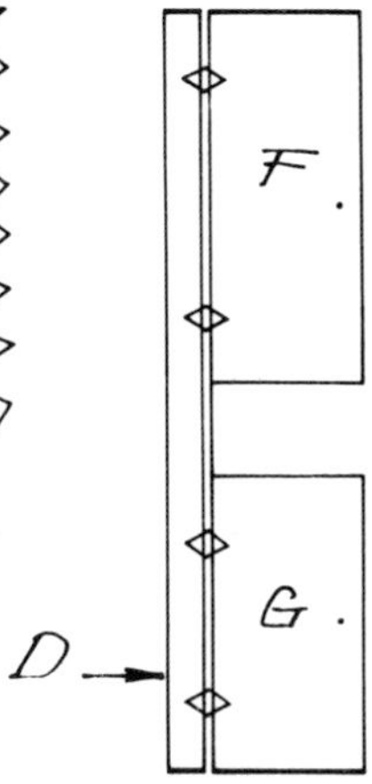

FIG. 6

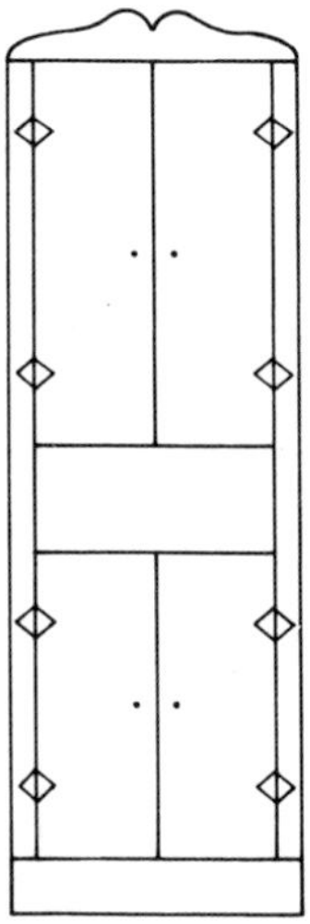

FIG. 7

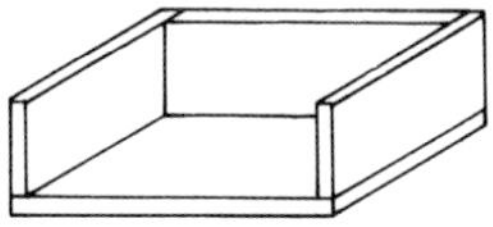

FIG. 8

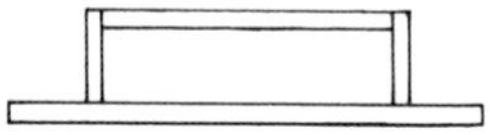

FIG. 9

CORNER CUPBOARD ASSEMBLY

4. Stain all pieces.

5. Run a thin line of glue along the back corners of both sides (A) at the 45-degree angle where the two sides will be joined together. It is a good idea to put one of the shelves in place at the bottom to insure the correct angle, but do not glue the shelf. Use a rubber band to hold it tight and allow the sides to dry.

6. Begin setting and gluing shelves (B) as in figure 3, starting with the top and working down. Be sure that all shelves are level and line up with the previously made witness marks. Glue the kick plate on at the bottom of the cabinet.

7. Glue the facing strip (E) in place (fig. 4). It should be placed on top, even with the front edge.

8. Lay the cupboard front facing strip (D) flat on your worksheet. Line the upper door (F) up with the top (fig. 5). A small opening (approximately $1/32$-inch) should be left between the two pieces of wood. Mark $3/8$ inch from the top and the bottom of the door. This is where you will place your hinges. Top hinge will be placed just below the top mark, the bottom hinge just above the bottom mark (fig. 5). Push a straight pin through to make the holes in the hinges. Glue each hinge in place, pushing a brad through the pre-punched holes in the hinges. Allow each hinge to dry (fig. 6). Repeat on the right-hand top door.

9. Repeat as above on the lower doors (fig. 7). There will be an opening for the drawer between the doors. Put a small dab of glue on a sequin pin. Put a 3-mm bead on the pin and push it through the doors. Using a pair of small wire snips, trim the hinge brads on the inside as close to the wood as possible. Also trim the pins.

10. Glue the back edge of (D) on the front edge of side (A). Set (D) into place. Repeat on the other side (fig. 7).

11. With the drawer bottom flat on the foil, glue drawer sides in place (fig. 8). Set drawer back between side pieces when dry. Center the drawer front in place (fig. 9). The drawer front will overhang the sides. Push 3-mm beads into doors, and trim the pins.

PAMELA WHITE'S ANTIQUE SEA CHEST

Materials
$1/16$-inch mahogany
Elmer's Glue-All
Epoxy
Stain
Varnish
2 brass hinges
2 brass handles
1 brass lock
$1/4$-inch strip of brass edging

Tools
Miter box
Small miter or dovetail saw (16 to 20 teeth to an inch)
Mat knife
Triangle
Ruler
Sandpaper
Wire cutters

Cut out all pieces of wood using a miter and saw except for the fitted corner joints of the bottom front. Use a mat knife for these. Fine-sand all pieces before assembly. In subsequent steps, where glue is used, wipe off excess with a rag and warm water before it dries.

LID ASSEMBLY

1. Cut the top of the lid, $1/16$ by $1\frac{1}{4}$ inches by $2\frac{7}{8}$ inches. (Cut correct size from $1/16$ by 2-inch wood since wood is not available $1/16$ by $1\frac{1}{4}$ inches.)

2. Cut two pieces for the long sides of the lid, $1/16$ by $1/4$-inch by $2\frac{7}{8}$ inches. Glue these to the underside of the lid, flush with the outside, so that you see the edge of the top from the side.

3. Cut two pieces for the short sides of the lid, $1/16$ by $1/4$-inch by $1\frac{1}{8}$ inches. Glue these to the underside of the lid, flush with the outside, also, of course, so that you see the edge of the top from the side.

4. Put a rubber band around the sides to hold them in place and set aside to dry.

BOTTOM

1. Cut the bottom of the bottom, $1/16$ by $1\frac{1}{8}$ inches by $2\frac{3}{4}$ inches.

2. Cut backside $1/16$ by $3/4$ by $2\frac{3}{4}$ inches.

3. Cut one front side, $1/16$ by $3/4$ by $2\frac{7}{8}$ inches but with $1/16$ by $1/2$ inch cut away from each end to provide a fitted joint with side pieces (fig. 3).

4. Cut two sides, $1/16$ by $3/4$ by $1\frac{1}{4}$ inches each with $1/16$ by $1/4$ inch cut away from one end to fit at right angles with front pieces (fig. 3).

5. Glue these four sides onto the outside edge of the bottom piece, and glue them to each other, making sure the fitted joints at the front are a smooth fit. You should not be able to see the bottom piece except from the bottom.

6. Put a rubber band around the sides and set to dry.

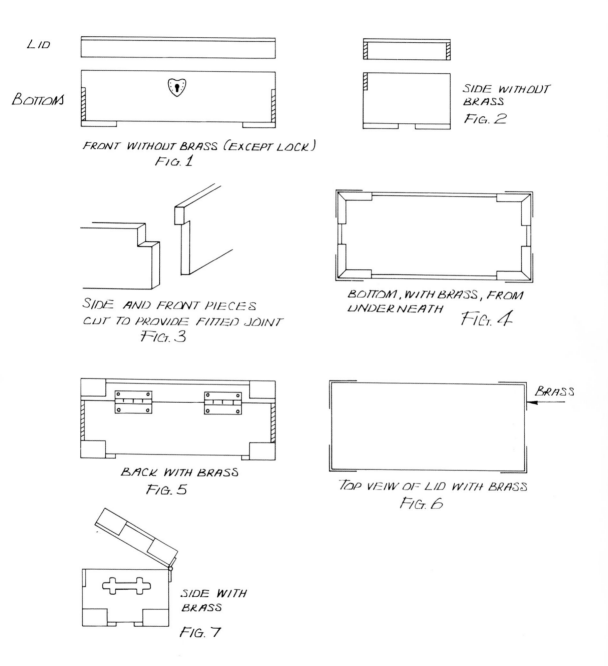

LID

BOTTOM

FRONT WITHOUT BRASS (EXCEPT LOCK)
FIG. 1

SIDE WITHOUT
BRASS
FIG. 2

SIDE AND FRONT PIECES
CUT TO PROVIDE FITTED JOINT
FIG. 3

BOTTOM, WITH BRASS, FROM
UNDERNEATH   FIG. 4

BACK WITH BRASS
FIG. 5

BRASS

TOP VEIW OF LID WITH BRASS
FIG. 6

SIDE WITH
BRASS

FIG. 7

7. When dry, cut eight $^1/_{16}$ by $^1/_8$ by $^1/_2$-inch pieces, each with one mitered edge.

8. Glue these corners to the bottom to serve as feet (fig. 4).

9. Fine-sand all outer faces of chest.

BRASS

1. With epoxy, glue one side of each hinge to the edge of the back of the lid's side, at least $^3/_4$ inch from outside edge of chest. Let dry.

2. Cut eight pieces of brass $^1/_4$ by $^3/_4$ inch and wrap it around all eight corners, gluing with epoxy. Make sure the brass is flush with the top and the bottom (figs. 5 and 6). To get a clean bend to the brass, score it lightly first with your knife along the bend line and bend it over a sharp, straight edge.

3. With epoxy, glue the handles to the sides of the bottom (fig. 7).

4. With epoxy, glue the lock on the front (fig. 1).

5. When the hinges have dried thoroughly, with epoxy glue the other side of the hinge to the top edge of the bottom side, thereby attaching the lid to the bottom. Make sure the hinge works properly and clean off the excess epoxy.

6. When the epoxy is dry, push brass pins through the holes in the hinges and cut them off as close as possible to the wood on the inside of the box. File the remainder of the pins level.

FINISHING

1. Stain the wood with either mahogany or walnut stain.

2. Varnish with a dull to semi-gloss finish.

3. Do not get the finish on the brass. You may, in fact, put all the finish on before gluing on any of the brass, except that epoxy works somewhat better on bare wood.

Basswood and brass are essential parts of Pamela White's New England sea chest.

Pamela White's Colonial chair has horizontal back slats and a seat of twine. (Marcia Fall)

BARBARA TAYLOR HACKNEY'S RUSH-SEATED CHAIR

Materials

⅛-inch pine dowel, 12 inches long
^{1}/₁₆-inch pine dowel, 12 inches long
⅛-inch pine strip, 16 inches long
Duco cement
Paper clips or thin wire
Coats and Clark's Speed Cro-Sheen mercerized cotton in wheat or brown or ^{1}/₃₂-inch twine
Paint or stain

1. Measure and cut the front and back legs of the chair from the ⅛-inch dowel, using accompanying pattern (figs. 1 and 2).
2. Mark turnings with a pencil and then file (fig. 3).
3. Cut the rungs for the bottom of the chair from the ^{1}/₁₆-inch dowel. Taper slightly each end of each rung.

4. Cut the vertical slats for the chair back from the pine strip (fig. 4). Sand smooth.
5. Cut the four pieces for the seat frame from the rest of the pine strip (fig. 5).
6. Stain and let dry unless you are planning to paint the piece. If you are, paint with a Colonial shade.
7. Glue the four sides of the seat frame securely.
8. With the point of one of your needle-nosed files, "drill" the holes you will need in the legs and stretchers, positioning the holes about ^{1}/₁₆ inch deep very carefully, following the pattern (fig. 6).
9. In the ends of the stretchers and back slats, insert cut-off pieces of paper clip or wire and set in with glue (fig. 6).
10. When wires or clips are glued solidly, insert back slats into holes drilled in stretchers.
11. Assemble and glue the entire front and back sections of the chair. Side rungs should be glued in later.

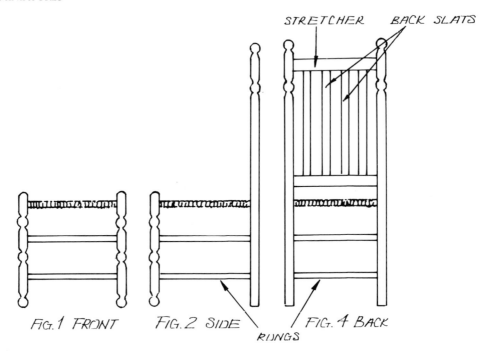

STRETCHER

BACK SLATS

FIG. 1 FRONT FIG. 2 SIDE FIG. 4 BACK

RUNGS

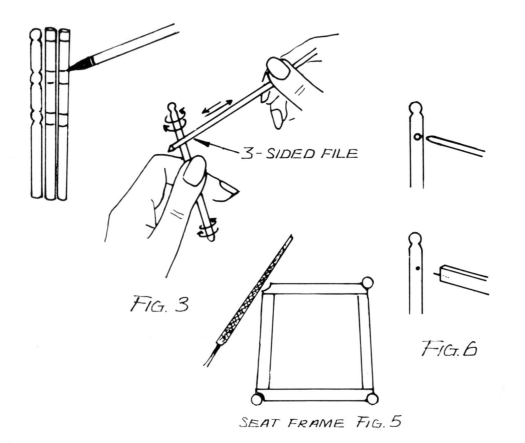

3- SIDED FILE

FIG. 3

FIG. 6

SEAT FRAME FIG. 5

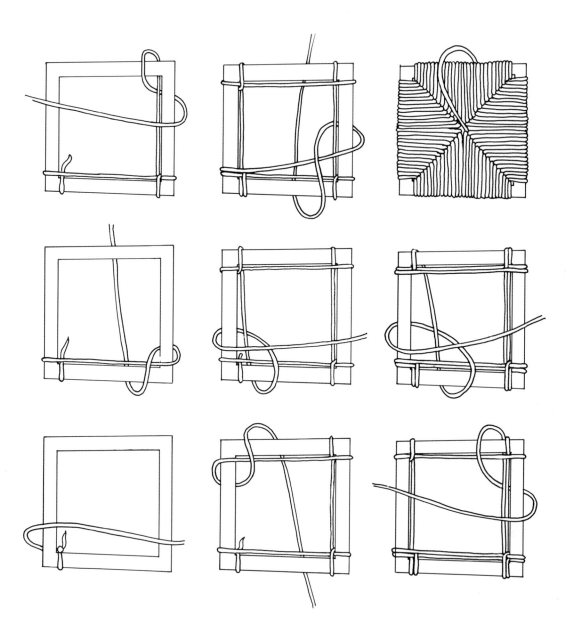

12. Now weave the seat with the yarn or twine. As you get close to the center (following pattern), it may be necessary to work with a needlepoint needle, and use the needle for weaving the ends into the bottom of the seat when you finish. The beginning piece can simply be woven under as you go over and under in the beginning. Be sure your yarn or twine lies flat and even as you go along. Some people like the look of shellac over twine if you choose to use twine. If that appeals to you, apply some shellac when the weaving is finished.

12. Work arcs with round file in the corners of the seat frame (fig. 5).

13. Finish assembling and gluing the rest of the chair, front and back, to seat and rungs.

CHAPTER 10

*High-button shoes like these Mitzi Van Horn
fashions might be on sale in your general store, too.
(Mitzi Van Horn)*

A GENERAL
STORE

❦ NOW YOU'RE a miniature-maker. You can fashion mouth-watering food, plates to serve it on, tables, chairs, candles, and all the accessories of gracious living. You can sew mini-afghans and hook mini-rugs. And you have a container—a dollhouse, an aquarium, a bookcase, a piece of driftwood, or a wooden box.

One of the most entertaining ways to fill a container is to make it a shop. If you're handy with needle and thread, try designing hats for a milliner's shop. If you have a sweet tooth but are on a diet, why not sublimate by filling a bakery with chocolate cakes and crusty French bread?

You might want to sell lobsters out of a fisherman's shack, or toys in a toy store, or tools in a hardware store. But if you're the eclectic sort who enjoys making a little of this and a little of that, try a general store. And when you go on to make room settings, you'll be amazed at how often you go shopping in your store.

A general store like this one that Elspeth creates provides all sorts of opportunities for the imaginative miniaturist. In it can go bolts of cloth, cards of buttons, a pot-bellied stove, dowels carved into barrels (or barrels made of cardboard), jugs that once were rubber cane tips. There's no end to the objects with which an able miniaturist can supply a general store.

COUNTER

To begin with, you will need a counter. Elspeth makes hers of matboard, gessoed and spray-painted. The one on the opposite page is made from ceiling molding.

1. Take a piece 2½ to 3 inches high, and glue a slightly longer, slightly wider strip of flat wood to the molding with Weldwood to form the counter top.
2. Stain it as you wish.

SHELVES

Elspeth makes her shelving of matboard, in the following way:

1. Cut matboard strips that are about the length of your room setting and an inch or a little more wide.

2. Cut matboard strips about the same width as the shelves to go between the shelves as vertical supports.
3. With Elmer's glue, attach shelves and supports to back wall.
4. Coat shelves and supports lightly with gesso and let dry. Antique them or not, as you choose. If the shelving buckles, Elspeth says, it can easily be straightened with the fingers when almost dry.

Shelves can also be made from squared-off tongue depressors, cut partway through and fitted together. Stain them and glue them to the setting with wood glue.

On a general store counter, you will need a cash register and a display case, and you might like a root beer dispenser and a gumball machine. Claire Danos of Ridgewood, New Jersey, makes all of these, as well as cigar and candy boxes and a potbellied stove.

CASH REGISTER

Materials

A quarter round piece of molding, 1 inch in radius, 1 inch long for the body of the register

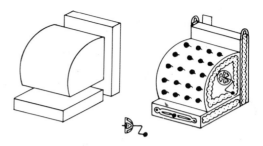

Three pieces of molding glued together make this counter. Microscope slides, half-round molding and jeweler's filigree, brads and a barrette are combined in this cash register by Claire Danos. Her gumball machine began with a plumber's female adapter and the plastic cover from a supermarket charm.

A block of wood less than ½ inch thick and slightly larger across than the molding for the drawer

Another block of wood less than ½ inch thick, 1 inch wide and slightly taller than the quarter round for the back of the register

Wire brads for keys

A microscope slide for the top

A bead cap, stiff beading wire or florist's wire and a glass or wooden bead for the handle

Filigree as decoration for the sides and back

A barrette for a front drawer decoration.

1. Assemble all pieces as shown, gluing wooden pieces with Weldwood or Titebond, the handle with epoxy.

2. Cut the filigree pieces so the design and the height will match each other on both sides. Glue them to the sides of the register with epoxy. Glue the front of the barrette to the drawer front.

3. Drill tiny holes with an X-acto drill in the front of the register to insert the brads (if you don't do this, you will split the wood).

4. Drill a small hole in the side of the register (where there is an opening in the filigree, of course) to insert the handle.

5. Spray-paint gold or black.

6. Now glue on the glass slide top with Weldit.

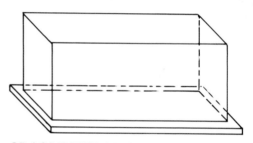

GLASS DISPLAY CASE

Materials
Three glass microscope slides
A wooden slat slightly larger than a slide for the bottom of the case
Weldit cement
A glass cutter

Use the full-size slides for the top and the front of the case. With the glass cutter, cut the third slide in two to make the sides. Glue all the pieces together. The back of the case remains open.

CANDY BOX

At holiday time—Christmas and Valentine's Day and Easter—even a general store dresses up a little and sells boxed candy as well as the penny kind.

To make a box of holiday chocolates:

1. Cut a small rectangle from gold craftboard or a lightweight gold-colored card. The exact size will depend on the poundage you're selling. It's all up to you.

2. Cut and glue in place low white cardboard sides and three cardboard dividers so your candies can be invitingly displayed in an open box on the counter.

3. If you prefer to protect your confections from dust and dirt, glue together a clear plastic cover.

CIGAR BOX

Cigar boxes are endlessly useful in miniature making. This mini-box also makes use of the real thing.

Round toothpicks cut in small pieces and painted fill this Claire Danos–designed cigar box.

Materials
1/16-inch gold craftboard
Elmer's Glue-All
Masking tape
Cigar-box wood
Cigar-box labels

1. Following the pattern, cut a rectangle of craftboard (A). The gold side will be the interior of the box.

2. Where the pattern is marked with broken lines, score the cardboard lightly with a razor blade or X-acto knife on the underside to facilitate bending.

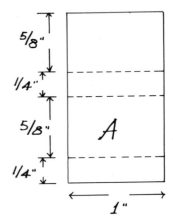

3. Cut a second piece of craftboard (B).

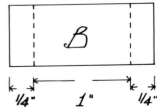

4. Lay the first rectangle on top of the second to reinforce the bottom of the box and, where the second piece is scored and bent, make the sides for the box.

5. Tape the rectangles together to form a box shape.

6. Now cut six pieces of genuine cigar-box wood a smidgeon larger than the craftboard pieces and glue them to the craftboard so your box has a real cigar-box exterior. Be sure all the grain of the wood runs in the same direction.

7. On top of the box, glue the gold designs from cigar wrappers and old cigar-box labels. (Flea markets sometimes sell them.) If you

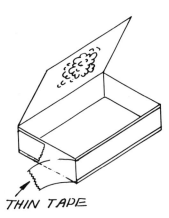

THIN TAPE

cannot find the labels already removed, buy cigar boxes and remove the labels by soaking them in warm water. Let them dry before affixing them. Save the leftover wood for other projects.

8. Bits of reed or round toothpicks painted cigar color and cut to fit the box will make your cigars.

GUMBALL MACHINE

Materials

A plastic charm cover (dome-shaped) of the sort that comes in supermarket gumball machines

The back of a large, round earring

The base of a female adapter from a hardware store

A bead to resemble a handle

A jewelry finding with a hole in it to "release" the gumballs

Colored sprinkles (for decorating cakes) for the gumballs

1. Hold the charm cover upside down. Put the sprinkles inside and glue on the other pieces as shown with Weldit.

2. Spray-paint the bottom. (Gesso the bottom first if you want a smooth look.)

CANDY

Without candy, a general store simply wouldn't be a general store. An assortment of delectably colored glass beads are hard candies. Flat beads in pastel colors are dandy thin mints. To turn beads into chocolate kisses, simply wrap them in Hershey kiss paper. Make jelly apples from pearls, spray-painted red with acrylic paint and glued on a round toothpick. (Pearls have an inviting shine to them.) Licorice is thin black tubing from an electronics shop.

CANNED GOODS

There must be canned goods on your shelves, and you can saw them from dowels. Look at the pictures on coupons that come in the mail. They often are in perfect scale for mini-canned goods and boxed goods and you can glue them to your "cans" of peas and peaches. Hearing aid batteries are also the right size for bigger cans, for instance cans of paint.

THREAD

To make the spools of thread that every general store carries:

1. Punch the tops and bottoms of the spools from a plain white index card, using a round ticket puncher.

2. Glue a bugle bead between the card-board rounds with Elmer's glue.

3. When the spool is dry, wind enough fine thread around it to fill it.

4. If you prefer genuine wooden spools, slice $1/16$-inch dowels to mini-spool size and glue and wind thread around them.

MATERIAL

To make bolts of cloth the way Susan Sirkis does:

1. Cut a wooden yardstick into 2-inch lengths.

2. To make artificial selvages on the material you use, draw two straight pencil lines on the wrong side of the fabric you will put on the bolt. The lines should be two inches apart and along the straight grain of the fabric. Run a thin line of Sobo glue along each pencil line. Let the glue dry, then cut along the lines.

3. Coat the pieces of yardstick with Bond-Grrip and wrap the material around it. Turn the outside edge under and glue it in place.

4. You can also use wooden dowels as the core for your fabric "rolls."

RIBBON

Susan Sirkis sells mini-ribbon in her general store on pieces of swab sticks cut to the width of the ribbon on hand. Wrap the ribbon round and round the stick and glue it in place.

BUTTONS

Cut little rectangles from the backs of Christmas cards and sew beads on the cards for your buttons.

SOAP

Elspeth makes soap cakes by melting the ends of candles and pouring them into a shallow container. Cut them into mini-laundry soap size while the wax is still warm.

For wrapped soap, look around again for labels on coupons and wrap tiny squares of balsa wood in paper decorated with these labels.

BROOM OR MOP

Your spick-and-span customers will certainly need a broom and a mop.

1. Use a swab stick as the broomstick, or a twig if your store is really old-fashioned.

2. Make the broom itself by winding light gold and yellow embroidery floss around a 3-inch square of file card. Slide floss off the card and cut the ends.

3. Glue the floss, with Elmer's, to the swab stick 1½ inches from its end. Fold the floss over and wrap with several other strands of floss as shown.

4. Flatten the broom with your fingers on both sides. Fashion it so it is the broom shape you wish. Lay it on wax paper and spray hard with an unscented, non-aerosol hair spray. Lay more wax paper on top and leave the broom to dry.

5. When it is thoroughly dry, trim the bottom even. The hair spray will harden the broom "bristles" so they are just like real bristles in miniature, assures Elspeth, whose design this is.

6. To make a mop, use beige embroidery floss or white string—but fewer strands, and forgo the hair spray.

MILK CAN

Spools painted silver with paper clips glued on for handles are excellent milk cans.

CIDER JUG

On a crisp fall day when a hot fire is blazing in the general store stove, and the cider has just been pressed, some of it will surely be on your shelves in a jug made from a chair leg tip or cane tip of rubber.

1. With epoxy, attach a small piece of wire for the handle.
2. Use a tiny rivet as the top, plugged with a mini-cork cut from a larger cork.
3. Gesso and paint with acrylics to resemble a cider jug. The bottom and top of the rubber tip should be beige; the rest dark brown.

BARRELS

How about cracker barrels so your customers will have a place to perch? Buy doweling a little larger in diameter than you would like your barrel to be and sand it to shape with coarse sandpaper.

PLUNGER

An essential item for a general store. B. Jean Silva of West Tisbury, Massachusetts, makes them from small dowels and the rubber caps that are at the end of orchid corsage tubes. *Sic transit gloria mini Mundi.*

SACKS

Make your coffee and flour bags of muslin. Check coupons that come in the mail for mini-labels. Fill the bags with flour or coffee or sugar (but beware of mice and ants finding your mini-setting too homey).

For mini-bags of flour and sugar, burlap or coarse linen may be used.

A fisherman's shack is a good place to use up a miniaturist's odds and ends. Fenner Wheeler put this one together. (Richard Benjamin)

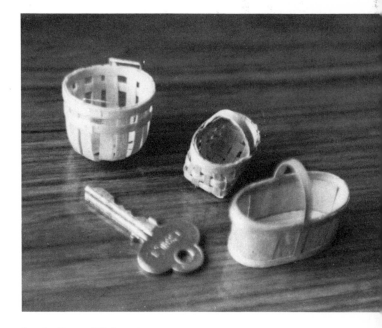

Carolyn Bugg of Wichita, Kansas, weaves
mini-baskets of all shapes.

A hat shop is attractive in miniature. This one was designed by Claire Danos. (George W. Carva)

HAT STAND

Press a candleholder into a papier-mâché craft ball of appropriate size. Turn upside down. Paint on the face with a ballpoint pen and the hair with a felt-tipped pen. Glue together a circle of felt, tiny flowers, veil, ribbon, whatever you wish on a hat, and then glue it, a trifle askew, on the hat stand. Use Elmer's glue.

Men's hats by Mitzi Van Horn would be a dashing attraction at any store. (Mitzi Van Horn)

FEATHER DUSTER

Wrap and glue a handle of beading wire around a collection of pillow feathers.

POTBELLIED STOVE

You simply couldn't have a general store without a potbellied stove.

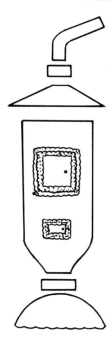

Materials
The cardboard tubing from the bottom of a
coat hanger (not all cleaners use tubing
for this purpose so you may have to shop
around till you find one who does)
A washer or grommet or flat round bead
A large bead cap or old brooch of a similar
shape
A Bufferin bottle
Flat, round beads
A large bead cap
A lace paper doily or filigree paper

1. Glue together two pieces (to make the bend) of tubing for the vent with Elmer's glue.
2. Glue pieces of lace paper doily all around the bottle for embossed design.
3. Glue all the other pieces together.
4. Glue on beads for knobs. Spray-paint the stove black.

A plastic medicine bottle, filigree, and the cardboard tube some cleaners use on their pants hangers were put together by Claire Danos to create a pot-bellied stove.

ROOT BEER CONTAINER

There is nothing so thirst-quenching as an old-fashioned root beer on a hot day. Claire Danos makes a container from a plumbing fitting (rummage around at your local hardware store until you find one that looks appropriate for the base) and a round glass medicine bottle that will fit into the plumbing fixture. As with the gumball machine, you might want to use a female adapter. Fill the bottle with sherry or other wine that is root-beer colored. Wine won't become moldy or cloudy with age as most other liquids will. With epoxy, glue on a jewelry finding or piece of wire for the spout. Spray-paint the bottom.

A Christmas tree of pipe cleaners is, of course, the center of attention in this festive room by Elspeth.

CHAPTER 11

At holiday time, a wreath provides a festive frame for a miniature setting. (Andrews Miniatures)

A CHRISTMAS ROOM

🐇 Miniatures make endearing gifts for any occasion. With your new hobby, it is conceivable that you may never have to shop for a present again. Almost anyone would treasure a gift made with the meticulous and loving care that goes into the fashioning of precise and tiny objects.

Of all occasions, though, miniatures seem most suited to Christmas, and a Christmas room, for a very special person or family, is a treasure to be enjoyed year after year as it is set up anew each Christmas morning.

Begin this project by selecting a container. Paper the walls and finish the floors (or frame your setting the way Joe and Jackie Andrews do with a Christmas wreath). Whatever your container, the focal point of the room will be:

THE FIREPLACE

Here are several fireplaces to choose from. All of them have one thing in common—a black, sooty interior. To achieve this used effect, paint the inside of your fireplace with a flat black paint, and then rub a little white acrylic over the black. You wouldn't want a fire on the night Santa is expected, but you might decide that yours is a Christmas *morning* room, and then a fire would be just the thing. To make it, cut red and yellow cellophane into "spurts" and glue them to logs made from twigs.

COLONIAL FIREPLACE

A simple wooden picture frame makes the front of this fireplace. The frame should be about 1½ inches wide. Use your miter box to assure neat corners and cut one 5-inch piece for the top and two 4-inch pieces for the sides of the front. Glue the pieces together with Elmer's glue, using your square to square the corners properly.

To box in the sides and back of the fireplace, use thin basswood. Cut a 4 by 5-inch piece for the back and two 1 by 4-inch pieces for the sides. Coat the pieces with airplane dope. Then glue them to each other and to the face of the fireplace with Elmer's.

The mantel is also made of basswood. Cut the piece 1⅛ by 5¼ inches—this will allow for a ⅛-inch overlap in front and at each end.

This simple Colonial fireplace looks well painted off-white. If you like, you can add a Colonial carving in the shape of a medallion or an escutcheon. Make it from jewelry findings. Paint the decoration gold or white and glue it to the fireplace with Duco cement.

You can make a similar fireplace by using ½-inch miniature molding. See the chapter on sources.

TILED FIREPLACE

After you have made your fireplace according to the directions above, you can decorate it with Delft tiles. Buy a sheet of Delft tile miniature paper and cut three strips of tiles to surround the fireplace opening. Apply the paper with wallpaper paste. To create the shiny look of genuine tile, paint the strips of paper with three coats of clear varnish.

BRICK OR STONE FIREPLACE

The fireplace photographed below is by Agnes Miri of Ridgewood, New Jersey. Before you begin, collect the main materials:

A rectangle of marble 6 inches long, 2½ inches wide and ¾ inch high. (If you are ready to give up before you begin, don't—the base of a bowling or other trophy is the perfect size and shape. If holes remain after you remove the trophy, they will be covered by the fireplace. Or if you don't want to dismantle your trophy, you may be able to buy a base where trophies are made.) The marble block will be the base of your fireplace.

Cigar-box wood.

Bricks or stones. Make the brick chips you will need by wrapping a real brick in a towel or rag and chipping at it with a hammer. Or if you prefer stone, chip from white stone used for garden paths.

Titebond glue

Minwax mahogany stain

1. Cut two pieces of the cigar-box wood 5¾ inches wide by 3 inches high. Put one of the pieces aside; this one will be the back of your fireplace. With a hacksaw, cut an opening in the other piece for the fireplace. Make the opening 2 inches high by 3 inches wide.

2. Cut a mantelpiece 1⅝ by 6¼ inches. This will give you a ⅛-inch overlap in the front of the fireplace and a ¼-inch extension on each side.

3. Cut two pieces 3 inches high by 1¼ inches wide for the sides.

4. Glue these pieces, including the front, together with Titebond glue. When the piece is dry, glue to the marble base. When that glue has dried, carefully stain all the wood with Minwax mahogany stain.

5. To lay the bricks, spread Titebond all over the front piece and set in your bricks or stones.

Turn to chapter 6 for instructions on how to make a screen, andirons, and tools for your fireplace.

A bowling trophy base is the hearth of this stone fireplace below by Agnes Miri of Ridgewood, New Jersey. The fire screen is made from an unrolled metal hair curler.

STOCKINGS

Cut the stockings that are "hung by the chimney with care" from felt and decorate them with tiny sequins.

Try beads for a miniature Christmas wreath. (Peter Schaaf for Mini Mundus)

WREATH

And, of course, you want a wreath for the wall. Here is how Dorothy Lindquist makes hers:

Wrap fuzzy green elastic gift wrapping cord around the ring of a shade pull. Attach little red beads with a needle and thread or with glue. Make a bow from a thin strip of red ribbon cut from a larger ribbon.

Or Susan Sirkis cuts green felt into a ½-inch strip, 2 inches or so long, depending on what diameter she wants for her wreath. Sew a strip of embroidery floss down the center of the length of the felt. Gather and knot it. Then twist this strip round and round the thread to make a ruffle. Sew the ends together into a wreath shape and glue on clusters of red berries with Bond Grrip. If you use longer strips of felt, you can make garlands this way, too.

You can also make a wreath by stringing green beads on jeweler's wire.

ORNAMENTS AND DECORATIONS

Run thread through bits of broken Styrofoam to make strings of popcorn.

Make candy canes from red and white television hook-up wire or from red and white striped sandwich bag closers. These are easily twisted and shaped into cane form. Cut them to size.

Cut gingerbread men from tan leather gloves (if you like soft gingerbread) and sew or paint on beadlike eyes. If you prefer gingerbread that is crisp, cut your gingerbread men from cardboard and decorate them.

Festoon your tree with delicate gold chains or strings of tiny bright beads.

Pretty beads strung on jeweler's wire make Christmas tree ornaments. Use as many beads as you like—a small one at the bottom, a large one in the middle and perhaps a prism-shaped one at the top. When you have as many beads as you want, cut off the wire at the top, leaving enough to loop the ornament over a branch. Claire Danos recommends crystal beads with a gold design on them.

To make a single bead-ball ornament, twist fine wire, looped double, tightly enough to go through the ornament. Twist the wire at the bottom so the bead will stay in place (or use a little glue). Leave wire at the top to form a loop. This is the way Barbara Hackney makes her Christmas ornaments.

You can make hand-dipped candles for your tree (see Accessories chapter) or use the tip end of a round toothpick. Dip the toothpick in gesso. Make the holder from a small cylindrical bead and a flat bead. Glue them and the candle together and the whole thing to a branch.

Use aluminum foil to make tiny angels and stars and cornucopias that can be filled with bright bead candies.

At Christmas time, look into your jewelry box as Barbara Taylor Hackney did to decorate this little tree. (J. Kender)

THE CHRISTMAS TREE

Elspeth makes hers from five packages of green pipe cleaners, an 8-inch piece of ¼-inch dowel and a 2-inch square of plywood that becomes the base.

1. Glue and nail the dowel to the base.

2. Then, starting at the bottom of the tree, twist six pipe cleaners around the bottom. Half of each cleaner should be twisted on one side of the tree, half on the other. Hold the "branches" in place with Elmer's glue.

3. Continue attaching the rows of cleaners up the tree, but cut each layer shorter as you near the top. Twist shorter lengths of pipe cleaners around each branch as you progress to give a "natural look."

4. Cover the wooden base with a white cloth to resemble snow.

Beads may be used effectively in many Christmas decorations. (Peter Schaaf for Mini Mundus)

GIFTS

WRAPPED PACKAGES

It wouldn't be Christmas morning if there weren't packages under the tree. Cut "boxes" from balsa wood and wrap them in foil or gilt paper or regular wrapping paper that has a mini design. Tie them with brass or silver beading wire or one strand of embroidery floss. Touch the floss with Elmer's glue to stiffen it a little and allow it to dry before you tie the "ribbon" around the package.

TOYS

Put some unwrapped gifts under the tree, too—maybe a miniature yarn doll or a teddy bear fashioned from Sculpey.

Doll   Elizabeth Fisher makes a cherry pit or a yew berry doll by stripping the paper from a sandwich bag tie, bending the wire in two to form body and legs and closing the bend tight enough so it will go into a hole drilled with a No. 60 drill bit into a yew berry or cherry pit and will not wiggle. Wrap the body and legs with ordinary white store string or crochet cotton. Under the head, attach an additional piece of wire for the arms. Wrap it, as well, with cotton or string. Clothe the doll as you choose and paint her face and hair.

Drum   Cut a small piece from a dowel. Paint the sides red with acrylic paint, the top and the bottom white. Paint the strings on the drum with India ink. Snippets of copper wire will do as drumsticks.

Of course, you'll want some very important gifts, too. Here are some especially nice ones.

Jack-in-the-Box   A jack-in-the-box like the one made in Belmont, Massachusetts, by Terri, a skilled miniaturist who specializes in games and sporting goods and nursery items would also brighten Christmas morning.

1. Cut a $^1/_{16}$-inch piece from a $^1/_4$-inch dowel for the crown of the hat.

2. Cut a thin sliver from a $^1/_2$-inch dowel or use a large black sequin to make the rim of the hat.

3. Find a $^3/_8$-inch wooden bead—about the size of a large blueberry—for the head.

4. For the collar, you will need a fluted sequin about $^5/_8$ inch in diameter.

5. Remove the spring from an old ball-point pen for the spring to attach Jack to his box.

6. To make the box itself, cut a $^1/_2$-inch square of basswood, or use a square wooden bead. You will need a small piece of $^1/_{32}$-inch basswood from a hobby shop for the lid, or white cardboard. (If you want a working Jack-in-the-box, make a small box and attach the top with a tiny hinge. At the front, have a hook catch.)

7. Glue all these pieces together with Sobo. Glue the lid to the back of the box. Drill a hole in the top of the solid box almost to the box bottom. Into this, glue the spring. If you find that the spring is too large for the hole you have drilled, enlarge the hole slightly with a file.

8. To decorate Jack's face, drill a small hole where you want the nose to be. Cut most of the pin off a round-headed straight pin that has a bright red bead end and glue it into the hole. Draw the rest of the face with a felt-tipped pen.

Dollhouse   1. Cut all the pieces for your house from $^3/_{16}$-inch sheets of basswood. The front of the house should be 2 inches high by 3 inches wide; the roof should be 3⅛ inches across and 1¼ inches high; the ground floor 2¼ by 3 inches and the two top floors 2 by 3 inches.

2. Cut the openings for windows with an X-acto knife. With slivers of basswood, make mullions and glue them in place with Elmer's. Cut a place for the front door. Glue molding strips around the window openings and glue in a door.

3. Paint walls, ceilings, and floors with acrylic paint (or paper the wall pieces with the tiny patterns found on dress pictures in catalogues, and stain the floors, if you wish).

4. If you would like lights in your minihouse, glue them to the walls or ceilings. Use beads glued into bead caps.

5. Glue the three floors to the front of the house, leaving ¼ inch of the ground floor extended in front. Then glue on the sides and the roof.

6. Cut sandpaper to fit over the roof and glue it to the roof. Paint it red or brown.

7. Glue on a stick of wood to represent the chimney.

8. Cut strips of white file cards or paper for the shingles, and basswood to make tiny shutters. Glue shutters and shingles in place.

9. Cut Q-Tips to fit as pillars for the front of the house and glue them between the roof overhang and the ¼-inch piece left on the ground floor.

10. Fill with balsa wood furniture.

A sandpaper roof and Q-Tip pillars grace this mini-dollhouse for a dollhouse, designed by Agnes Miri of Ridgewood, New Jersey.

Room Divider If you have a Florentine leather glasses case buried in a drawer somewhere, make it into a decorative room divider screen for the mother of your mini-setting. Cut two pieces of balsa wood to the same size; hinge them together with brass hinges from a hobby shop. With Elmer's glue, mount the leather on the balsa wood. On the edge of the wood, glue strips of gilt paper. On the back, glue clear plastic like that used in photo albums.

Telescope How about a telescope for Dad? Two pieces of small brass tubing fitted inside each other, with the "case" painted with dull black paint, will make one.

Agnes Miri uses cigar-box wood and Q-Tips for a playpen.

PLAYPEN

Since the baby of the miniature family will be playing under the tree on Christmas morning, it would help to have a playpen there for him. Make it from cigar-box wood and the long Q-Tips used for throat cultures.

1. Cut two 3-inch squares from the wood. Cut out the center of one square with an X-acto knife so that all you have left is a ½-inch rail for Baby to hold on to. In cutting, make sure that your corners are really square. (If you prefer, you can make a rail from ¼-inch strips of spruce, 3 inches long, with mitered corners. Glue these pieces with Titebond. If you use this technique, you will need only one 3-inch square of cigar-box wood, for the bottom of the pen.)

2. Lay the top rail on the bottom square and drill holes through both pieces around the edges. The Q-Tips will be inserted into these holes. The Q-Tips should be 2½ to 3 inches high.

3. Stain all pieces with Minwax mahogany stain.

4. Insert Q-Tips in the bottom holes. Glue them into the rail holes.

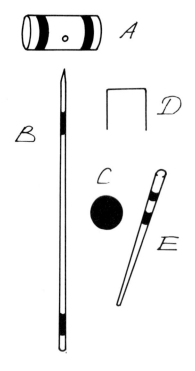

Croquet Set What about looking toward summer with a Christmas gift of a croquet set? Terri offers these instructions:

1. Make the mallets (A) of ¼-inch dowels cut into six ½-inch pieces. Drill a tiny hole in the center of each. Cut off toothpick points and insert them (B) in these holes. They should be cut so that after they are inserted the handles are two inches high. It may be necessary to cut off the toothpick head to get a snug fit. Glue them with Sobo.

2. With Testor's paint or acrylics, paint rings in different colors around the base and handle of each mallet—red, yellow, blue, green, orange.

3. To make the balls (C), plug the holes of six round ¼-inch wooden beads with filler. Paint each ball a different bright color to match the rings painted on the mallets.

4. You can make wickets (D) from ⅜-inch heavy-duty staples or from 22-gauge wire bent into a wicket shape.

5. To make stakes (E), cut two 1-inch sections from a round toothpick. Each toothpick will make two stakes. Paint stake tops in bright stripes.

6. Use ¹/₁₆ by ¼-inch strips of basswood for the stand. Cut these into two 2-inch pieces, two 1¼-inch pieces, two 1-inch pieces and two ³/₁₆-inch pieces. Glue the 1¼-inch and the ³/₁₆-inch pieces together with Sobo, using the short pieces on the ends to make a box (H) for the mallets to rest in. Glue the 2-inch pieces (F) onto the back of the box ¼ inch from each end (G).

7. Drill a hole in each of the 1-inch pieces (G) (they will be the feet of the mallet stand) ¹/₁₆ inch from the edge to accommodate the stakes.

8. Make the ball channel (J) of ¹/₁₆-inch basswood just wide enough to accommodate the balls and 1⅞ inches long.

9. Glue the 1-inch feet to the 2-inch uprights, leaving the drilled hole to the back.

10. Now make a second channel ⅛ inch wide and 1 inch long (K) and glue it to the two uprights and the feet. This will serve a dual purpose. It will provide space for the mallet handles and also make a stronger glue joint for the uprights and feet.

11. Center and glue the ball channel in front of the ⅛-inch channel. Spray or paint with enamel or lacquer.

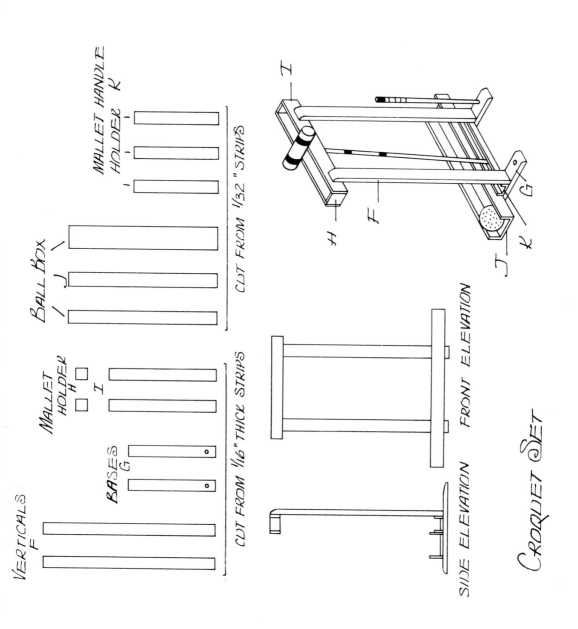

MALLET HANDLE HOLDER K

BALL BOX

CUT FROM 1/32" STRIPS

MALLET HOLDER

BASES G

VERTICALS F

CUT FROM 1/16" THICK STRIPS

FRONT ELEVATION

SIDE ELEVATION

CROQUET SET

Rocking Horse Surely a toddler would appreciate this rocking horse fashioned by Fran and Bob Cook of La Mirada, California:

Materials

⅛-inch wood—bass, fir or pine
1/16-inch doweling or round toothpicks
    with the points cut off
Leather scraps
6 inches of string or yarn
Elmer's Glue-All
Sandpaper
Toothpicks for applying glue, paint or
    stain
Aluminum foil to use as a worksheet

1. Cut the pieces according to pattern, drilling holes where shown. Leg and neck holes are drilled at an angle. Rocker supports, rein, and tail need straight-drilled holes.
2. Smooth the surfaces of the seat, the head, and the rockers with sandpaper, rounding the edges.
3. Stain or paint the pieces.
4. Insert legs (E) into four corner holes of seat (A) and glue them in place. They should be flush with the top of the seat.
5. Rocker supports (D) should now be fitted into the inside holes of the rockers and glued.
6. The neck (F) should now be inserted and glued into hole in the underside of the horse's head (C).
7. Allow all parts to dry thoroughly. The legs and neck should extend at an angle. When all the pieces are dry, insert and glue the legs into place in holes on top of rockers (B) and the neck into the hole at the center of the front of the seat.
8. Knot an end of the string or yarn and pull it through the hole for the tail at the rear of the seat. Put a second knot in the tail about 1 inch from the seat and fray the ends of the tail.
10. Apply the leather ears (cut from scraps) to the sides of the head with glue. Paint the eyes and the bridle as you choose.
11. Draw a 4-inch length of string or yarn through the hole in the horse's jaw and bring it around to the center of the seat. Knot and trim it for reins.

A rocking horse and a coloring book belong under every Christmas tree.

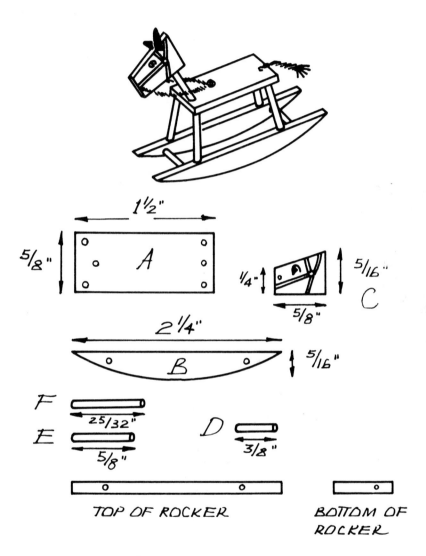

1½"

5/8"

A

¼"

5/16"

C

5/8"

2¼"

B

5/16"

F

25/32"

E

5/8"

D

3/8"

TOP OF ROCKER

BOTTOM OF ROCKER

MELL PRESCOTT'S ROCKER

Beside the fireplace on Christmas Day, piled high with the teddy bears and the candy boxes, there should be a comfortable rocking chair. Master miniaturist Mell Prescott of Warrenville, Connecticut, makes this one:

1. Cut wood according to pattern. Cigar-box or balsa wood will do nicely for sides and seat. Only rockers and arms will show. These should be cut from maple, walnut, or mahogany. Stain.

2. Glue the rockers onto the side pieces with Elmer's glue. Make sure the chair rocks evenly.

3. Cut the back from shoebox cardboard.

4. From pure wool coat material or an old blanket, cut a 5 by 10-inch piece for the cushion and chair back.

5. Glue the sides, back, and seat of the chair together.

6. Glue the cushioning wool to the back and the seat of the chair (applying a thin layer of glue to both the wool and the wood and cardboard surfaces). Use two thicknesses of wool at the top and bottom of the back, but only one thickness at the middle.

7. Glue the paper patterns of the back and sides on the gingham or calico you have selected. Cut out the material, but leave about ½ inch extra at the top of the side pieces to go over the back. The back piece should fit exactly.

8. Glue the material to the wood and wool. Make the "ruffle," marking the pleats as they are in the picture. (Use selvage for the pleats.) Glue on the ruffle. Then glue on ⅛-inch-wide (or less) braid. If you cannot find braid in a color that complements your fabric, dye white braid. When you are gluing, apply the glue directly to the braid.

And there you are. Merry Christmas!

Mell Prescott of Warrenville, Connecticut, is the designer of this comfortable rocker and June Dole of Rockville, Connecticut, cross-stitched the sampler.

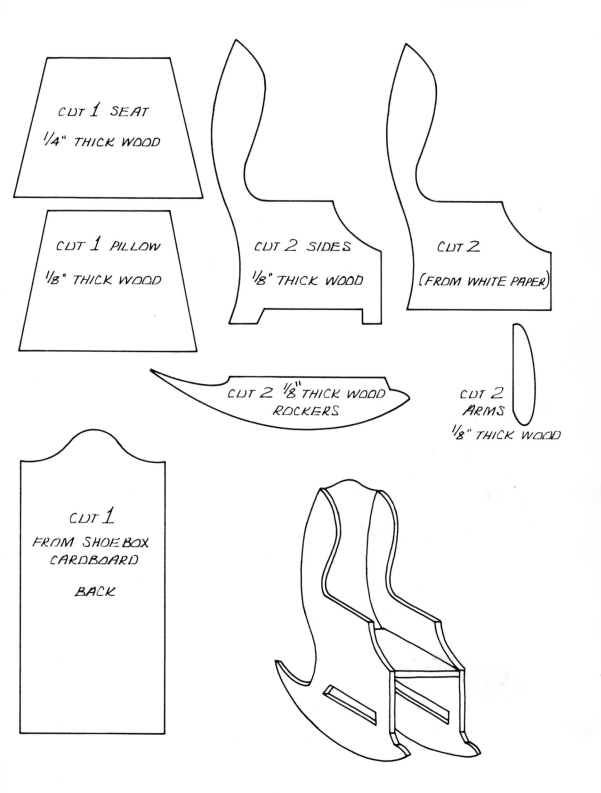

CUT 1 SEAT
1/4" THICK WOOD

CUT 1 PILLOW
1/8" THICK WOOD

CUT 2 SIDES
1/8" THICK WOOD

CUT 2
(FROM WHITE PAPER)

CUT 2 1/8" THICK WOOD
ROCKERS

CUT 2
ARMS
1/8" THICK WOOD

CUT 1
FROM SHOE BOX
CARDBOARD

BACK

Odds and ends of jewelry findings, tube and bottle caps, and a toothbrush make this assortment of tiny accessories conceived by Barbara Taylor Hackney. (J. Kender)

CHAPTER 12

A mini-banquet can be held at a table like this one, made by Donald Buttfield. (Photography Unlimited)

HOW TO MAKE MONEY FROM MINIATURES

❧ Skillful miniaturists, having satisfied their own needs—after all, how many petit point rugs, or sets of china, or birthday cakes can you use?—may discover they have a hobby that pays off in money as well as pleasure. It takes little space, a minimum of tools, and doesn't call for a great investment in materials. If your candied apples have a melt-in-your-mouth appeal, you can simply set up shop in a corner of the kitchen, and when the children are at school, paint pearls from a broken necklace into candied apples. At New York's Mini Mundus (an antique toy store that became a miniature shop when the owner's astrologer told her she would soon be dealing in small things), candied apples bring more than $1 for three; bread-dough cantaloupes are upwards of $.25 apiece, and chocolate cakes start at $2.

If you're handy with jewelry findings, spend your Saturdays at flea markets. One miniature-maker got $36 worth of lamps out of a $4 "junk" necklace last summer. The summer before, she sold 375 "Gone With the Wind" lamps made from jewelry findings and made enough money to pay for a two-week vacation.

You must bear in mind, however, that miniature-making demands patience, good eyesight, and devotion. "You can make money at it, certainly," says Evelyn Gerratano of Trumbull, Connecticut, who paints miniature china, "but you mustn't do it unless you love it. Some days, with all the work I put into a piece, I don't make more than fifteen cents an hour."

Dorothy Lindquist knits on straight pins, and her mini-knitting sells for more than $2, but the work that she does is so tiny, and must be done with such care, that she can only prepare three mini-knittings a night. (A "complete" mini-knitting is about a half-dozen rows of work-in-progress.)

But if you love little things, have time and talent, and want to be a mini-maker, you can make money at it.

ARE YOU GOOD ENOUGH?

Before you do anything else, find out how good your work is, and if it seems salable. Miniature collectors are almost always perfectionists, enthralled by tiny things made exactly like bigger ones but with that extra fineness that reduction in scale from 1 foot to 1 inch requires.

All across the country, shops are selling miniatures, both mass-produced and hand-crafted. Look for miniatures in gift shops, antique stores, toy stores, department stores, shops that sell handcrafts and shops that deal only in miniatures. Expert estimates are that shops specializing in miniatures have been opening at a rate of more than 1000 a year since the current craze for collecting and making miniatures began.

Take your work in to one of these stores and ask for an evaluation. If you're good, you may end up with a dealer then and there. If you show promise, but haven't quite made the grade yet, a friendly shopkeeper should be able to advise you about improving your work. Or he can tell you if some other product would be more salable than what you're making.

Robert von Fliss, the editor of *Miniature Gazette*, and himself a maker and seller of miniatures, told of two young men who came into his shop with a handsome modern dollhouse they had made. "It was beautifully done, but miniatures are a nostalgic thing. Victorian is especially popular in our part of the country now, so I told them to try their hand at that. They came back with a beauty that I sold for five hundred and fifty dollars. I sold nine more of them after that, till they got tired of making dollhouses."

"If what you make in the miniature line has quality, the world really will beat a path to your door," Mrs. Harold Appleyard, a New Jersey dealer, maintains. She recalls the woman who stopped hesitantly at her shop one afternoon to ask Mrs. Appleyard what she thought of her petit point rugs. "They were simply unbelievable," Mrs. Appleyard says, "and of course we began carrying them."

PUBLICATIONS

One dealer may be all you can supply, but if you want to establish a larger market, a good way to go about it is to advertise in the miniaturists' publications—*Nutshell News*, the *Miniature Gazette*, *Dollhouse and Miniature News*. If you make only one or two specific items, name them in your ad. If you offer a variety, it is probably better to announce that hand-molded food or needlepoint or mini-pottery is what you do, and ask your potential customer to send $.25 (and a self-addressed, stamped envelope) for a price list. If you offer an illustrated catalogue, you could charge $1 or more. Charging for catalogues, of course, helps to defray the cost of printing.

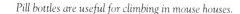

Pill bottles are useful for climbing in mouse houses.

If you have so many ideas for miniatures that you would be up day and night making little things if you made them all yourself, an alternative is to sell patterns or directions and let other people pay you for the privilege of doing the work. Advertise in one of the national publications. One especially able and imaginative young woman grosses more than $20,000 a year with such patterns. She started by writing a column of advice to miniature-makers. Then she borrowed money from her husband to print several collections of patterns. She sent postcards about them to her friends and found there was enough interest to warrant printing more; now she has average sales of 5000 patterns a year. She keeps records of everyone who buys a pattern and notifies them when the next book of patterns appears.

Another way to make money from miniatures is to sell kits—for dollhouses, furniture, metal accessories, petit point, or whatever you make best. You pack up the materials the miniature-maker will need (thereby saving a search on the other end for supplies that may be hard to buy retail), prepare a set of instructions and diagrams where necessary, and package the kit for mailing. Set a good price on your kit, and, again, advertise it nationally.

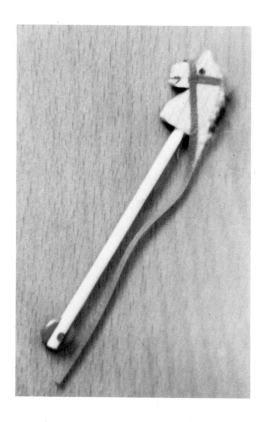

This little hobby horse is made by Isn't It in Tulsa, Oklahoma. (Concord Depot)

SHOWS AND SALES

The National Association of Miniature Enthusiasts (NAME), holds eight major shows and sales a year, and many local shows as well, and it is not unusual for a maker of fine furniture to gross $3000 in one weekend. Simple, well-made furniture—Shaker and Colonial—begins at about $10 for a piece. More complicated pieces like Victorian and Queen Anne, are $50 and up.

A first-rate accessory maker, whose items range from $.50 to $20 may average $1500 at a good show and sale.

At last year's Milwaukee NAME "house party"—so called because miniaturists are concerned with mini-houses and their contents—one buyer spent $100 in just a few hours on nothing but odds and ends for her dollhouse. In Ashland, Virginia, at another houseparty, a newcomer to collecting spent $1000 in three days. Longtime collectors are a good deal less extravagant, but $100 is the average expenditure by people who attend the major miniature shows and sales. These are held in Annaheim, California, Boston, Cleveland, Philadelphia, and Huntington Beach, California. Other communities holding shows of increasing prestige are Ashland, Virginia, Bridgeport, Connecticut, Long Beach, California, and Tulsa, Oklahoma.

To sell your wares at a show, you have to rent space, which may cost $25 or more for a half table. You also have to pay $15 to $20 in registration fees, the cost of a hotel room, and transportation to the convention. (If you want to do this, be sure to check on show dates in miniaturists' publications well in advance, and sign up for them. At one Boston show, all dealers' space was booked within a month of the announcement. Even many of those who simply wanted to attend couldn't get in. One dealer, who isn't taking any chances about being left out, signs up for shows as long as three years in advance.)

If show arrangements are more than you can manage, there are many dealers who regularly go to shows and are often willing to accept items from other miniaturists. Sometimes they work on a commission basis; sometimes they buy objects outright for resale. Some of the busiest of these are the Woman's Exchange in Hingham, Massachusetts, which handles the work of twenty craftsmen; Paige Thornton of Atlanta, Georgia; the Appleyards of Linwood, New Jersey; and Mr. and Mrs. Joseph Andrews of Ashland, Virginia. There are about a dozen major dealers in the nation.

Still, an increasing number of craftsmen do their own selling at these affairs because—despite the expense and problems of transportation and bookings—they are in better control of sales if they do it themselves. Because a master craftsman is limited in the number of goods he can make in a given period, he is likely to set a correspondingly reasonable limit on the number of future orders he takes for particular items. A dealer may not be quite so conscious of this problem.

All dealers in miniatures advise the beginner not to try to sell his work at church and county fairs, general craft shows, and mall shows. "You'll simply get trampled by the seeker of macrame and hand-thrown pots. Passersby will undoubtedly exclaim 'Oh, how cute' as they finger your six-inch cannonball bedspread and dirty the creamy ecru. But the kudos and fingermarks rarely equal money," one dealer points out. "To sell miniatures, go where the collectors are," she advises.

Ed Whitten of Southboro, Massachusetts, makes this rocker and Wee'uns of Hingham, Massachusetts, the pillow. (Concord Depot)

Mary Carraher uses toothpicks for the back of her Windsor chair.

Place mats should be made of the thinnest available material, edged with a cross-stitch.

Miniatures from the Depot Gallery, Concord, Massachusetts. (Gerald Ashby)

Wall hanging or rug—this heraldic creation in petit point will do for either. (Peter Schaaf for Mini Mundus)

SPECIALIZING AND EXPANDING

With the current enthusiasm for miniatures, a talented craftsman may often find that he has more work than he can handle. Gretchen Deans of New Canaan, Connecticut, who makes dollhouses for dollhouses, (they sell for more than $50), went to a show with her houses and was "discovered" by a dealer. Now she has all she can do to keep the dealer supplied. Another designer, who makes a miniature doll for a dollhouse, can scarcely fill her mail orders even though the doll sells for $100. A Pennsylvania craftsman who has been making crockery less than six months has orders that amount to $70 a day.

To be a success, it is important, as Bob von Fliss points out, to make what the collectors want. The designer of miniatures for Terri's Workshop in Belmont, Massachusetts, echoes his sentiments. "If I made tables or chairs or Victorian stuff," she says, "forget it—everyone is doing that. So, since I'm a sports nut, I thought I'd try a sporting line." She designed tennis rackets, pool tables, croquet sets, golf bags—even crutches for broken-limbed mini-football players—and placed ads in publications for miniaturists. Within three months, she had cleared more than $2000.

But don't count on making a living with miniatures unless you are free to spend all your time at it. Unless you go commercial and hire assistants, you're unlikely to be able to produce enough to make more than $10,000 a year—and even that will mean pretty tired eyes and sore fingers, says Dorothy Lindquist. "Doing one hundred of one item isn't bad," she says, "doing two hundred is all right, but six hundred is horrible!"

OPENING YOUR OWN BUSINESS

If you have a big house, in an area zoned for cottage industry, you may decide to forgo any other shop or dealer and open your own business in your living room. That's assuming, however, that you don't mind a parade of visitors day in and day out. One craftswoman, even though she only allows shoppers to come to her home by appointment, says the day is rare when she has time to eat lunch before 3 P.M., and she's likely to be showing off her handiwork as late as eleven at night. "I love it because the people who collect miniatures are such wonderful people to meet," she says. All the same, both you and your spouse and children have to be sociable sorts to enjoy the at-home shop. Establishing a shop outside your home is not likely to be profitable unless you become a dealer. Shop rentals are high, in general, and you're better off selling by mail order.

Even if you don't own your own shop, miniature-making often turns into a family affair. A wife may upholster or paint the furniture a husband makes; a daughter will take to cross-stitching samplers or painting mini-landscapes; a son may turn to making miniature metal items. Gaye Berry of Bozeman, Montana, started to make miniature upholstered furniture a few years ago. When business bustled beyond what she could handle alone, she talked her son into working with her. John Blauer, who was making room settings at his Miniature Mart in San Francisco, began to correspond with Ellen Krucher about the miniature china she made at her Peddler's Shop in Independence, Missouri. Soon they were married, joined businesses in San Francisco, and brought the bride's mother, a mini-coverlet-maker, into the business, too.

Polyform is the material B. Jean Silva of West Tisbury, Massachusetts, uses for this pottery.

This sink adds an old-fashioned flair to any mini-setting.

TEACHING AND LECTURING

With more and more people interested in both collecting and making miniatures—the interests increasingly overlap—some able craftsmen augment their income with teaching and lecturing.

Local NAME clubs often have workshop sessions at their meetings, or in private homes. Sometimes shops—Mini Mundus in New York and the Woman's Exchange in Hingham, Massachusetts, among them—offer classes. Adult education programs are beginning to offer courses in miniature-making.

If you are good with words, you can go on the lecture circuit. You may or may not be paid to speak, but the chances are that your expenses will be paid, at least. And if the occasion at which you've been asked to lecture is a big NAME houseparty, you'll be able to sell your crafts as well as talk about them, meet with your friends and competitors, and see what's new in the ever-growing world of miniatures.

A Colonial candlestand is a popular Ted Norton piece. (Richard Benjamin)

A mini-print ruffled bedspread like the one Elizabeth Sweet of Franconia, New Hampshire, makes will go well in any little room setting. (Marcia Fall)

This simple settee helps furnish Jane Crouch's keeping room.

A leather-topped table is one of the more elegant pieces of furniture youthful craftsman Rob Lyon makes.

CHAPTER 13

All set for the players are this gaming table and chairs by Donald Buttfield. (Photography Unlimited)

MASTER MINIATURISTS

Anyone can learn to make miniatures. That's what this book is all about. You don't have to be an artist or a carpenter, a potter, or a seamstress. There are former plumbers, bartenders, insurance men, photographers, secretaries, nurses, engineers, construction workers, businessmen—even doctors and lawyers, among miniaturists today. And many of them are at the top of the craft.

Ted Norton, a dean of miniature-furniture-making, used to be a plumber. Donald Buttfield ran his own excavating company until two years ago. Today, you can buy his six-inch copy of an eighteenth-century cherry secretary for $1200. The miniature world's leading glass blower is a Massachusetts Institute of Technology physicist whose specialty is the miniaturization of optical components.

Some of these master craftsmen, once they turn their abilities to miniature-making, give up their full-time occupations. Others fear they'll lose the pleasure that comes with their fine craftsmanship if they depend on it for a living, so they retain their jobs. But weekends and after dark they clear off the kitchen table, or go down to the cellar to do their handcrafting.

Harry Smith makes hundreds of objects in miniature, including this Queen Anne highboy. (Harry Smith)

The highest-priced miniatures being made in this country today are painstakingly turned out by Donald Buttfield in Fair Haven, New Jersey, and by Harry Smith, a dark-eyed, dark-haired former artist who lives in Camden, Maine. Both men were led to miniature-making by their wives—in one case purposefully, in the other quite inadvertently.

Nancy Buttfield knew, as her husband neared fifty, that he longed to quit the world of yawning earth-eaters for something quieter.

"He needed more perfection in things. He had done a little full-sized cabinetmaking to help fill empty corners in the house, and he had always liked building ship models. I felt those talents should be used. I knew Shirley Temple Black was collecting miniatures, and I thought if she was, there must be others. I got all excited about how maybe Don could make miniatures. I guess it was just luck."

Buttfield began making miniatures on vacations and weekends. He fashioned a grandmother clock after one he had seen in Williamsburg, Virginia, and a table and a chair and took them to a shop selling miniatures for an evaluation. They advised him to take them to Abercrombie and Fitch in New York, which he promptly did. Simultaneously, he exhibited his work at a crafts fair and won a blue ribbon. He gambled, sold his earth-moving business and became a full-time miniature-maker. At a show just a little time later, he sold $3000 worth of his work in one day.

Harry Smith's career in miniatures began in Chicago twenty years ago when he was sick in bed and his wife gave him a kit to make a scrapbook with a basswood cover. Instead of using the wood for the cover, he carved a deacon's bench with his pocketknife. As soon as he was up and about, he collected stones and made a fireplace to go with the bench. Marshall Field's bought those early pieces and told him they would like to see more. He enjoys fashioning 7½-inch japanned highboys of pine and butternut, lacquered with black and decorated with gold leaf (they sell for $1150). "Each miniature piece I make becomes a challenge and I insist that every one I make must be better than the last." He has been so successful that he has more than 7000 collectors as customers, and visitors come to see him at work from as far away as Paris.

Equally highly respected by the collectors is Ted Norton, who took to miniature-making when he developed a bad back crawling in and out of small openings as a plumber. He had made a dollhouse for one of his three daughters when she was young. His mother, an inveterate collector of fine china and glass, and a woman with a special fondness for miniatures, had always thought his dollhouse was exceptional. She urged him to try miniature-furniture-making. Today, Ted Norton can barely keep up with the orders for his handsome Queen Anne tables and chairs, his sideboards and candlestands and rocking horses.

Ted Norton of Westbrook, Connecticut, made this furniture and the setting. (Richard Benjamin)

Since her husband had made all the furnishings for the Andrews' full-scale house, she, like Mrs. Buttfield, proposed that he try making little pieces. "His little dining room table goes through exactly the same process when he's making it that my big dining room table did."

Mrs. Andrews, too, has become a miniature-maker, fashioning accessories; she also works as a dealer.

Robert Birkemeier of Manlius, New York, an executive of the Boy Scouts of America, had a neighbor who collected miniatures. They captivated him, and he tried carving a few pieces. (Making model airplanes was his only previous miniature-making experience.) He discovered he liked copying the furniture in his house, and his wife liked helping him—staining and finishing it and decorating the Boston rockers. Soon their son started making metal objects in miniature and their daughter was doing miniature paintings. Like the rest of the top-flight miniature-makers, the Birkemeiers find they can't keep up with the orders, particularly for the spinning wheel of thirty-seven turned pieces and their gaily painted rocking chair.

The United States Bicentennial Society honored Joseph Andrews of Ashland, Virginia, the office manager for a stained glass company, by making him one of its authorized licensees, selecting him for the high quality of his work. Once again, it was a wife's urging that led him to this income-producing hobby.

Jacqueline Andrews always loved tiny things and has long collected antiques in miniature. ("I have one of the loveliest dollhouses anyone could own," she says. "It's a replica of the thirteen-room Victorian Virginia house where I was born. There are seven hundred feet of siding and 2994 pieces in the shutters alone, and twenty-nine windows that go up and down, and it's filled with antiques.")

Robert Birkemeier fashioned this spinning wheel of many moving parts.

It's not only men who are attracted to miniature-furniture-fashioning. Twenty-five years ago, Betty Valentine's hobby was rush-seating chairs. After she ran out of full-sized chairs, she started making miniature ones with rush seats. When she discovered that making the chairs was so much fun, she decided to build and furnish a whole dollhouse. And when the dollhouse was finished and furnished, she still wanted to make miniature furniture.

"In those days," she remembers," there was a famous dealer in miniatures in Chicago named Joe Grey. I wrote to him and asked if he'd like to see any of my work. By this time, I was referring to Wallace Nutting's *Furniture Treasury* and other books on old furniture when I did my pieces, and I was measuring everything and scaling it down. Mr. Grey took the first piece I sent, and everything afterwards."

When he died, Mrs. Valentine did not know where to turn for another market and gave up miniature-making for a while. She got a job as a secretary but found it lacked the satisfaction she got from making things. She went back to miniature-making in the hope that she would eventually find other sales outlets.

She was living in Woodstock, Vermont, at the time, and the Rockefeller-financed inn there took some of her eighteenth-century miniature furniture for its gift shop. Catherine MacLaren, the editor of the miniaturists' publication *Nutshell News*, saw the pieces and mentioned them in a column. "The orders began to pour in," Mrs. Valentine recalls. Today she lives in Manchester, Connecticut, and says, "It's all just gotten away from me. I'm swamped with mail. I know I ought to answer it, but if I do, that's time I'm not making miniatures."

Mell Prescott of Warrenville, Connecticut, got into miniature-making quite accidentally. An expert flower arranger, one day she found herself in need of a miniature cradle to use as a container. Instead of giving up the idea when she couldn't find a cradle, she bought some tools and made her own. And soon she was making other pieces. Her children were amused at their mother's sudden interest in dollhouse furniture—until an architect offered her $500 to furnish a model of a house he was designing for a client. After

A cosmetic jar or a pill bottle, jewelry findings, a drawer pull, and filigree will make this miniature woodstove. This is a Claire Danos design.

*Mitzi Van Horn's work in metal includes dinner
gongs and candlesticks.*

Hepplewhite is a favorite style for Joe Andrews.

that, a moving company asked her to make miniature furniture with which they could teach their employees how to pack a van.

Today, Mrs. Prescott is especially known for her upholstered Victorian pieces. She uses silk fabrics bought in San Francisco's Chinatown for her fine upholstery and gingham in tiny patterns for ordinary pieces. She dyes her own trimmings. On some pieces, she works in conjunction with Ted Norton, who does the woodworking so she can concentrate on upholstering.

Among the leading petit point makers of the miniature world is Mitzi Van Horn of Richmond, Virginia. The first miniature objects she made were ceramics for an eighteenth-century apothecary shop. Since she had no experience with pottery, she began to visit a friend with a kiln and learned how to make full-scale objects from her. Then she turned to miniature jars and fine china sets. Once she was adept at those, she learned to make miniature metal objects; then furniture; then petit point. Next, she was doing Bargello-upholstered miniature chairs. "I know I dibble and dabble," she says, "but it's so boring to do the same thing over and over!"

A surgeon's wife, she doesn't make her living at miniature-making, and wouldn't want to "because there's no way you can even make the minimum wage if you do a quality product. It takes me ten days just to do the needlework on the little upholstered chair I sell for eighty-five dollars."

Martha Farnsworth, the wife of a California judge, is another petit-pointer (though she calls her work "petit" petit point because it is so fine that to be properly viewed it must be examined with a magnifying glass). In addition to doing petit petit point rugs and wall hangings—only on order—she sells patterns by mail order and at conventions of miniaturists. In odd moments, she hand-embroiders and hand-rolls the hems for the sheets in her thirteen-room dollhouse.

Betty Rockoff, another California miniaturist, specializes in food. In the pattern of collectors who turn creators when they can't find what they need, she couldn't find food that looked like food. So she began sculpting miniature baked hams and heads of lettuce and chocolate cakes of wax or ceramic. The choice of material depends on which most

realistically forms the product. Friends liked her work and urged her to sell it. She's never advertised, although she is listed in books of miniaturists and sends out a flyer with photographs of the foods she makes. Her mostly word-of-mouth reputation is such that last year she was so swamped with orders she was forced to cut down on the number of creations she offers. She now makes only three dinners—one for a Thanksgiving or Christmas table that includes a turkey with a slice cut out, cranberry sauce, pumpkin pie, Brussels sprouts, and yams; a New England dinner of boiled beef, potatoes, beets, carrots, onions, and cabbage; and a baked ham dinner "that is really pretty tricky to make because of all those little cloves all over." The cost of gourmet food in the mini world is high, and these dishes, which fit nicely onto your own little silver platters, begin at $12.

Occasionally, Mrs. Rockoff will still make wedding cakes, decorated with as many as forty handmade roses. (At this writing, the cakes are selling for $30.) She is now planning to combine wax and clay in an elaborate party cake "so I can get a nice, clean, glazed jelly look on top, or maybe a soft-looking chocolate frosting. Of course, each layer will be filled and textured. Texture is terribly important in foods."

Nothing is beyond Betty Rockoff's powers of creation in wax or ceramic. She makes crinkled raisins smaller than a pinhead and bowls of clay nuts with some of the nuts open and the membranes and nutmeats showing. A friend who was building a nineteenth-century dollhouse wanted a proper period cake for her kitchen. Since there was no baking powder in those days, the cake had to be fairly flat, so Mrs. Rockoff made a study of the height of cakes in the pre-baking-powder period before she created her miniature.

She talks of the making of ice cream for a miniature setting like an artist. "You mustn't just make it a glob. Real ice cream is dull where it's solid and shiny where it's melting."

A genuine business in hand-done ceramics has been established by Barbara Epstein of Dayton, Ohio, under the firm name Microbius. Like so many other miniaturists, she began creating for her own collection.

"I simply couldn't find dishes," she remembers. "I had no experience at all mak-

*A picture frame can add depth to your miniature set-
ting, the way this one does to Elspeth's Twiggtown
general store.*

ing pottery, but I went to the library and took
out a book on making molds and then I was
given a kiln as a birthday present. I'd never
seen one before but I started to use it. Of
course it was all trial and error at first, but
then it worked."

A New York collector and dealer, Robert
Milne, saw some of the early porcelain that
she made in miniature and suggested that she
advertise in publications for miniaturists.
Now requests for her work are so numerous
that she has had to hire other craftsmen to
help fill her orders.

"A lot of people order whole sets of china,
and that can be an enormous amount of
work," she says. Her four-piece place settings
average about $13. But for "Royal Worces-
ter," the price can go as high as $25. A
custom setting of a Chinese Export pattern
might be $35—or $420 for a service for
12—without the extra serving pieces.

In Convent Station, New Jersey, Deborah
McKnight, the wife of a Bell Telephone
Laboratories physicist, was tempted a few
years ago to take a course in pottery. "She
made that usual ghastly pot that everyone

makes," her husband recalls. "And then one
day she started making small things and discovered she had a real feeling for them."

Always fond of antiques, she began making
crockery that looked as if it were antique—
pitchers and bowls and pots and jugs. And
one day she got together a display case of her
items and took them to the neighboring
Morristown Museum, specializing in American art.

"She was so embarrassed at what she was
doing," her husband says, "that she pre-
tended she was the agent of someone she
named C. M. Small." But there was no need
to be embarrassed. The museum displayed
her wares readily, and soon miniature collectors were knocking at her door. Today, like
all good miniaturists, she cannot keep up
with the demand for her product.

In addition to crockery and porcelain
(she's made a Bicentennial plate that sells for
$10), Deborah McKnight makes birdhouses
and hanging clay pots. She still makes miniatures for the museum, fills orders at shows,
and looks after her husband and two
children.

"But I love having her making these things," her husband says. "I can't help wondering what size the people two thousand years from now will think we were when they dig up one of Debbie's little lobster dinners or a miniature apple core!"

In the field of metal, Al Atkins is generally considered the outstanding miniaturist. For years, Atkins made his living as a commercial artist. But the idea of blacksmithing had always appealed to him. "So I went to the library and began reading crumbling old books on it. They were full of dire warnings that said you must strike the anvil three times at midnight on Saturday to keep away the evil spirits on Sunday." They also were filled with concrete directions on smithing. Atkins bought his own anvil and began following the directions.

The first pieces he made were full-scale candlesticks and hooks and hinges, which he sold to a local gift shop. When a shop customer who was a miniature collector, but could never find the metal miniatures she wanted, asked him if he had ever thought of making any, he quit art to become a full-time blacksmith of miniatures. Now Atkins makes spiral staircases and jails with locking cells, and handcuffs and leg irons. He's even made flatirons for a miniature Chinese laundry.

Good glass blowers, making large objects or small, are hard to find, for glass blowing, increasingly, is becoming a lost art. When Agneta Domascewicz of Pembroke, Massachusetts, found she needed relaxation after her long, hard days as an M.I.T. physicist, she tried to take up mini-glass-blowing. But there was no one to instruct her. And even finding someone to teach her the technique of blowing full-scale glass proved difficult. When she finally found a teacher, mastering glass blowing took her two years.

Although the glass blowing she does today is primarily for her own use, she always makes an extra piece or two that she is willing to sell—chandeliers and goblets and little bowls of colored glass fruit.

Most miniature-makers are relatively new to the business—ten or a dozen years almost makes them old-timers. But Eugene Kupjack of Park Ridge, Illinois, has been fashioning tiny pieces ever since the 1930s when Mrs. James Ward Thorne commissioned him to do work for her miniature rooms, now the Thorne Collection at the Art Institute of Chicago.

A convention display and stage set designer when Mrs. Thorne found him, Kupjack devoted himself to the Thorne Rooms for three and a half years, until World War II began and he joined the navy. When he returned to civilian life, it was to the surgical instrument business. But his heart was in miniatures, and it wasn't long before he was making them again.

The mini-sterling silver he designs, and for which he does the master patterns, include copies of Paul Revere teapots and punch bowls; there are knives and forks and spoons and fish forks. He also makes a chess set with gold-plated pieces, and a $110 chandelier (somewhat apologetically he explains that the chandelier costs that much because "it's quite large. It weighs three and a quarter ounces.")

Miniatures are art, indeed, when they come from the hands of master craftsmen.

Buttons and beads, pins, chains, findings, and clasps are all components of many miniature accessories.
(J. Kender)

CHAPTER 14

sources

In the adage of the miniature-maker, "It's not what it is, but what it seems to be," and objects in the real world may never look quite the same to you again. The components of miniatures are everywhere you look. Hardware stores, grocery stores, drug stores, flea markets, jewelry stores, electronics and TV repair shops, supermarkets, dime stores, florist shops, antique shops, and, of course, craft and hobby stores, all offer items readily transformed to a special use by the alert miniaturist.

But of course there are also companies that manufacture with the needs of the miniature-maker distinctly in mind. Here are some of the best of these and the products in which they specialize. For information about their catalogues (most of which cost $2 and up) send a self-addressed, stamped envelope with your query.